The
CIVIL WAR
BOOK
of
LISTS

Over 300 lists, from the sublime... to the ridiculous

Compiled by the editors of
COMBINED BOOKS

CASTLE BOOK**S**

This edition published in 2004 by

CASTLE BOOKS ®

A division of BOOK SALES, INC.
114 Northfield Avenue
Edison, NJ 08837

This book is reprinted by arrangement with
Da Capo Press,
a subsidiary of Perseus Books L.L.C.
387 Park Avenue South
New York, New York 10016-8810

Originally published by
Combined Books, Inc.
151 East 10th Avenue
Conshohocken, PA 19428

Library of Congress Cataloging-in-Publication Data
The Civil War book of lists/compiled by the editors of
Combined Books.
   p.   cm.
Includes bibliographical references
1. United States—History—Civil War, 1861-1865—Miscellanea.
2. United States—History—Civil War, 1861-1865—Statistics.
I. Combined Books (Firm)
E468.C624   1994
973.7—dc20   94-33233   CIP

NOTE: *Union units are listed in italics throughout the book.*

ISBN 0-7858-1702-6

Printed in the United States of America

CONTENTS

4. Casualties

5. Generals

6. Troops

7. Society

8. After the War

9. The Civil War Today

INTRODUCTION

Americans have come to view facts in terms of numbers and lists more than ever before. The immense variety of lists available in everyday life tells us about the mood of the nation, the whims of fashion and reduces technical details into easily digestible information. The once dull practice of culling statistics has now become a popular form of information which has found a permanent home in today's mass media. This turn of events can of course be either benign or detrimental to the public at large depending on one's point of view. Certainly, the instant access to information through lists can increase public awareness. At the same time, however, reducing everything to facts and figures can transform even the most significant issues and events into impersonal numbers and data.

Numbers can often have a more serious impact than words if the reader takes a moment to ponder their implications. *The Civil War Book of Lists* is a cruel reminder of this fact. This book offers the opportunity to view the Civil War with the widest scope possible, to gain a full understanding of the nature of the country that went to war, the composition of the armies that took to the field and the battles that were fought. But the most lasting impact is the bloody cost incurred by the fighting that took place from 1861 to 1865. The butcher's bill was immeasurably high in terms of the cost of life during the war for Union and states' rights. The immense price the nation paid for the Civil War is laid out in these pages, not in mere numbers but in lives. Lists covering the bloodiest battles, the units which suffered the highest casualties and deaths by disease. These figures cut like a knife through the trite romanticism that still influences modern studies of the war.

The Civil War Book of Lists investigates other aspects of the War

THE CIVIL WAR BOOK OF LISTS

Between the States as well. Its editors have sifted through the dustbin of history to illuminate facts and figures about the war in a format that is as enlightening as it is easy to understand. The lives of generals, the deeds of soldiers and civilians and the weapons of destruction are detailed here, along with facts on economic, social and cultural issues. But the historian, buff or layman can not dine on numbers alone to understand this momentous and destructive period in American history. An extensive readers' guide offers the opportunity to select the best and most informative books from the mountainous numbers of texts available on the war. The editors have also taken the opportunity to have some modest fun with some of the figures that have become larger than life. Thus lists covering strange hairstyles, the ugliest generals and generals notorious as womanizers have been included in the text.

The object of the editors of Combined Books was to create a compendium of facts beneficial to the Civil War scholar. However, most of the interesting information is not in the works of the best-selling authors or the ivory tower offices of the leading professors, but in the studies and minds of the guerrilla historians and hobbyists out in the trenches of historical research. The editors of Combined Books make a special appeal to these individuals for comments, ideas and possible lists for a future publication. For this purpose, please address:

Civil War Book of Lists
Combined Books
151 East 10th Avenue
Conshohocken, PA 19428

CHAPTER 1

ARMIES

Confederate Units

Ten Best Confederate Brigades

1. Hood's Texas Brigade
2. Stonewall Brigade (Virginia)
3. Orphan Brigade (Kentucky)
4. Stuart's Virginia Cavalry Brigade
5. Hays' Louisiana Tigers
6. Lawton's Georgia Brigade
7. 1st Missouri Brigade
8. Gregg's South Carolina Brigade
9. Rodes' Alabama Brigade
10. Liddel's Arkansas Brigade

Ten Best Confederate Regiments

1. 1st Texas Infantry
2. 4th Virginia Infantry
3. 27th Tennessee Infantry
4. 6th Alabama Infantry
5. 9th Kentucky Infantry

6. 1st Virginia Infantry
7. 4th North Carolina Infantry
8. 44th Georgia Infantry
9. 18th Alabama Infantry
10. 17th South Carolina Infantry

Union Units

Ten Best Union Brigades

1. *First Vermont Brigade (VI Corps)*
2. *Iron Brigade (I Corps)*
3. *Irish Brigade (II Corps)*
4. *First New Jersey Brigade (VI Corps)*
5. *Excelsior Brigade (III Corps) (New York)*
6. *Philadelphia Brigade (II Corps)*
7. *Belknap's Iowa Brigade (XVII Corps)*
8. *Custer's Michigan Cavalry Brigade (Army of the Potomac)*
9. *Heckman's "Star" Brigade (XVIII Corps)*
10. *Steedman's Brigade (IV Corps)*

Fox's Fighting 300

This list is taken from William F. Fox's monumental study *Regimental Losses in the American Civil War* published in 1898. The regiments mentioned here lost 130 troops from deaths or deaths from wounds. While casualty figures are not necessarily proof of fighting quality, there is, perhaps, no better way to judge the ability of fighting units from the Civil War.

State	Regiments
Connecticut:	*2nd Heavy Artillery, 7th, 10th, 11th, 14th*
Delaware:	*1st*
Illinois:	*8th, 9th, 11th, 12th, 20th, 21st, 22nd, 30th, 31st, 34th,*

36th, 39th, 40th, 42nd, 44th, 48th, 55th, 73rd, 82nd, 84th, 89th, 93rd, 104th

Indiana: 6th, 9th, 14th, 19th, 20th, 22nd, 27th, 30th, 31st, 32nd, 38th, 39th, 40th

Iowa: 2nd, 3rd, 5th, 6th, 7th, 9th, 13th, 15th, 22nd, 24th

Kansas: 1st

Kentucky: 3rd, 5th, 6th, 15th, 17th

Maine: 1st Heavy Artillery, 3rd, 4th, 6th, 7th, 8th, 9th, 16th, 17th, 19th, 20th, 31st

Maryland: 1st, 6th

Massachusetts: 1st Heavy Artillery, 1st, 2nd, 9th, 10th, 11th, 12th, 15th, 16th, 19th, 20th, 21st, 22nd, 25th, 27th, 28th, 32nd, 34th, 35th, 37th, 54th (Colored), 56th, 57th, 58th

Michigan: 1st Cavalry, 5th Cavalry, 6th Cavalry, 1st Sharpshooters, 1st, 2nd, 3rd, 4th, 5th, 7th, 8th, 16th, 17th, 20th, 24th, 27th

Minnesota: 1st

Missouri: 11th, 12th, 15th, 26th

New Hampshire: 2nd, 3rd, 5th, 6th, 7th, 9th, 11th, 12th

New Jersey: 1st Cavalry, 1st, 3rd, 4th, 5th, 6th, 7th, 8th, 11th, 12th, 14th, 15th

New York: 1st Dragoons, 2nd Cavalry, 8th Cavalry, 10th Cavalry, 7th Heavy Artillery, 8th Heavy Artillery, 9th Heavy Artillery, 14th Heavy Artillery, 5th, 40th, 42nd, 43rd, 44th, 48th, 49th, 51st, 52nd, 59th, 61st, 63rd, 64th, 69th, 70th, 72nd, 73rd, 74th, 76th, 79th, 80th, 81st, 82nd, 83rd, 84th, 86th, 88th, 93rd, 97th, 100th, 106th, 109th, 111th, 112th, 114th, 115th, 117th, 120th, 121st, 124th, 125th, 126th, 137th, 140th, 142nd, 146th, 147th, 149th, 164th, 169th, 170th

Ohio: 5th, 7th, 8th, 14th, 15th, 21st, 23rd, 25th, 29th, 30th, 33rd, 34th, 36th, 38th, 41st, 46th, 49th, 55th, 65th, 67th, 73rd, 82nd, 98th, 127th

Pennsylvania: 7th Cavalry, 11th Cavalry, 5th Reserves, 8th Reserves, 9th Reserves, 10th Reserves, 11th Reserves, 13th Reserves, 11th, 26th, 28th, 45th, 46th, 48th, 49th, 50th, 51st, 53rd, 55th, 57th, 61st, 62nd, 63rd, 69th, 71st, 72nd, 76th, 81st, 83rd, 84th, 93rd, 95th, 96th, 97th, 100th, 102nd, 105th, 111th, 116th, 118th, 119th, 121st, 139th, 140th, 141st, 142nd, 143rd, 145th, 148th, 149th, 150th, 151st, 188th

Rhode Island: 2nd

United States: *1st Sharpshooters, 2nd Sharpshooters, 18th, 8th Colored Troops, 79th Colored Troops*

Vermont: *1st Cavalry, 1st Heavy Artillery, 2nd, 3rd, 4th, 5th, 6th, 10th, 17th*

West Virginia: *7th*

Wisconsin: *1st, 2nd, 3rd, 5th, 6th, 7th, 16th, 26th, 37th*

The Old Army

The Infantry Regiments of "The Old Army" Ranked by Seniority

1. *3rd Infantry*, formed 1789
2. *1st Infantry*, formed 1791
3. *2nd Infantry*, formed 1808
4. *5th Infantry*, formed 1808
5. *4th Infantry*, formed 1812
6. *6th Infantry*, formed 1812
7. *7th Infantry*, formed 1812
8. *8th Infantry*, formed 1838
9. *9th Infantry*, formed 1855
10. *10th Infantry*, formed 1855

The Artillery Regiments of "The Old Army" Ranked by Seniority

1. *1st Artillery*, formed 1821.
2. *2nd Artillery*, formed 1821.
3. *3rd Artillery*, formed 1821.
4. *4th Artillery*, formed—you guessed it!—1821.

Mounted Regiments of "The Old Army" Ranked by Seniority

1. *1st Dragoons*, organized in 1833, and redesignated the *1st Cavalry* in 1861.
2. *2nd Dragoons*, formed in 1836, becoming the *2nd Cavalry* in 1861.
3. *The Regiment of Mounted Rifles*, 1846, becoming the *3rd Cavalry* in 1861.
4. *1st Cavalry*, formed in 1855 and redesignated the *4th Cavalry* in 1861.
5. *2nd Cavalry*, also formed in 1855, becoming the *5th Cavalry* in 1861.
6. *3rd Cavalry*, formed in 1861, and being almost immediately redesignated the *6th Cavalry*.

The Generals of "The Old Army" Ranked by Seniority

1. Maj. Gen. Winfield Scott, Lt. Gen. by brevet.
2. Brig. Gen. David E. Twiggs
3. Brig. Gen. John E. Wool
4. Brig. Gen. William S. Harney

The States and Territories Ranked by Number of Active Militiamen in 1860

State	Militia Troops (Thousand)
1-2. New York	19.0
Pennsylvania	19.0
3. Virginia (C)	13.7
4. South Carolina (C)	7.0
5. Massachusetts	5.6
6. Ohio	5.5
7. Kentucky (B)	4.0

8-9. Mississippi (C)	3.0
Louisiana (C)	3.0
10-11. Alabama (C)	2.5
Tennessee (C)	2.5
12-14. Georgia (C)	2.0
Rhode Island	2.0
Wisconsin	2.0
15. Utah Territory	1.9
16-21. Arkansas (C)	1.5
Iowa	1.5
Minnesota	1.5
Missouri (B)	1.5
North Carolina (C)	1.5
Texas (C)	1.5
22-23. Maine	1.2
Michigan	1.2
24-30. California	1.0
Connecticut	1.0
Illinois	1.0
Kansas	1.0
Maryland (B)	1.0
New Hampshire	1.0
New Jersey	1.0
31. Vermont	0.9
32-37. Florida (C)	0.5
Indiana	0.5
Nebraska	0.5
Oregon	0.5
District of Columbia	0.5
New Mexico Territory	0.5
38. Delaware	0.2
39-43. Colorado Territory	0.0
Dakota Territory	0.0
Indian Territory	0.0
Nevada Territory	0.0
Washington Territory	0.0
Total	115.2

Numbers of Men Recruited for War

The States and Territories Ranked by Total Numbers of Men Recruited for the War Regardless of Side

State	Men	% Total
1. New York	448,850	11.7%
2. Pennsylvania	337,936	8.8%
3. Ohio	313,180	8.2%
4. Illinois	259,092	6.8%
5. Indiana	196,363	5.1%
6. Virginia (C)	192,924	5.0%
7. Tennessee (C)	166,227	4.3%
8. Missouri (B)	149,111	3.9%
9. Massachusetts	146,730	3.8%
10. North Carolina (C)	135,191	3.5%
11. Georgia (C)	133,486	3.5%
12. Alabama (C)	107,547	2.8%
13. Mississippi (C)	103,414	2.7%
14. Kentucky (B)	100,760	2.6%
15. Wisconsin	91,194	2.4%
16. Michigan	87,364	2.3%
17. Louisiana (C)	82,276	2.1%
18. New Jersey	76,814	2.0%
19. Iowa	76,242	2.0%
20. Maine	70,107	1.8%
21. Maryland (B)	66,638	1.7%
22. South Carolina (C)	65,462	1.7%
23. Texas (C)	60,012	1.6%
24. Arkansas (C)	58,815	1.5%

25. Connecticut	55,864	1.5%
26. New Hampshire	33,937	0.9%
27. Vermont	33,288	0.9%
28. At Large (US)	30,780	0.8%
29. Minnesota	24,020	0.6%
30. Rhode Island	23,236	0.6%
31. Kansas	20,149	0.5%
32. Florida (C)	17,334	0.5%
33. District of Columbia	16,534	0.4%
34. California	15,725	0.4%
35. Delaware	12,284	0.3%
36. Indian Territory	7,030	0.2%
37. New Mexico Territory	6,561	0.2%
38. Colorado Territory	4,998	0.1%
39. Nebraska	3,157	0.1%
40. Oregon	1,810	0.0%
41. Nevada Territory	1,080	0.0%
42. Washington Territory	964	0.0%
43. Dakota Territory	206	0.0%
44. Utah Territory	100	0.0%
Totals	**3,834,792**	**100.0%**

A "C" indicates a Confederate State, a "B" stands for a Border State.

The States and Territories Ranked by the Proportion of Population Furnished for Military Service Regardless of Side

State	% of Population	Number of Men
1. District of Columbia	22.0%	16,534
2. Kansas	18.8%	20,149
3. Nevada Territory	15.8%	1,080
4. Illinois	15.1%	259,092
5. Tennessee (C)	15.0%	166,227
6. Colorado Territory	14.6%	4,998
7. Indiana	14.5%	196,363

8. Pennsylvania	14.3%	337,936
9. Minnesota	14.2%	24,020
10. North Carolina (C)	13.6%	135,191
11. Arkansas (C)	13.5%	58,815
12. Ohio	13.4%	313,180
13. Rhode Island	13.3%	23,236
14. Mississippi (C)	13.1%	103,414
15. Georgia (C)	12.6%	133,486
16. Missouri (B)	12.6%	149,111
Combined Average	**12.4%**	
17. Florida (C)	12.3%	17,334
18. Connecticut	12.1%	55,864
19. Virginia (C)	12.1%	192,924
20. Massachusetts	11.9%	146,730
21. Wisconsin	11.8%	91,194
22. Michigan	11.8%	87,364
23. Louisiana (C)	11.6%	82,276
24. New York	11.6%	448,850
25. New Jersey	11.4%	76,814
26. Iowa	11.3%	76,242
27. Maine	11.2%	70,107
28. Alabama (C)	11.2%	107,547
29. Nebraska	11.0%	3,157
30. Delaware	10.9%	12,284
31. Vermont	10.6%	33,288
32. New Hampshire	10.4%	33,937
33. Texas (C)	9.9%	60,012
34. Maryland (B)	9.7%	66,638
35. Indian Territory	9.4%	7,030
36. South Carolina (C)	9.3%	65,462
37. Kentucky (B)	8.7%	100,760
38. Washington Territory	8.6%	964
39. Dakota Territory	8.0%	206
40. New Mexico Territory	7.9%	6,561
41. California	4.8%	15,725
42. Oregon	3.5%	1,810

43. Utah Territory   0.2%   100

44. At Large (US)   30,780

Totals   **3,834,792**

Recruiting totals as a proportion of total population are somewhat deceptive. On this list, for example, the first five areas listed included a large number of fugitive slaves among the total numbers of men recruited, troops who were not credited to their "home state" but rather to that which enrolled them.

A "C" indicates a Confederate State, a "B" stands for a Border State.

Numbers Recruited for Confederate Service

Military Population of Southern States in 1861

State	Military Population
Alabama	39,967
Arkansas	65,231
Florida	15,739
Georgia	111,005
Louisiana	83,456
Mississippi	70,295
North Carolina	115,369
South Carolina	55,046
Tennessee	159,353
Texas	92,145
Virginia	196,557
Total	**1,064,193**

The States in Order of Men Furnished for Confederate Service

State	Number	% of C.S. Army
1. Virginia (C)	155,000	15.0%
2. Georgia (C)	130,000	12.6%
3. North Carolina (C)	127,000	12.3%
4. Tennessee (C)	115,000	11.1%
5. Alabama (C)	100,000	9.7%
6. Mississippi (C)	85,000	8.2%
7. South Carolina (C)	60,000	5.8%
8. Texas (C)	58,000	5.6%
9. Louisiana (C)	53,000	5.1%
10. Arkansas (C)	45,000	4.4%
11. Missouri (B)	40,000	3.9%
12. Kentucky (B)	25,000	2.4%
13. Maryland (B)	20,000	1.9%
14. Florida (C)	15,000	1.5%
15. Other (Indian Terr) (B)	5,000	0.5%
Totals	**1,033,000**	**100.0%**

Regional Summary

Border States	90,000	8.7%
Confederacy	943,000	91.3%

Confederate recruiting records are even more incomplete than those for the Union. Figures here include men who served as militia or state troops, as well as those regularly enlisted in the Confederate Army. In addition to the states and territories indicated, small numbers of men from other areas also enlisted, but no separate records were maintained.

A "C" indicates a Confederate State, a "B" stands for a Border State.

The States in Order of Proportion of Population Enlisted in Confederate Service

	% of Population	Number
1. North Carolina (C)	12.8%	127,000
2. Georgia (C)	12.3%	130,000
3. Mississippi (C)	10.7%	85,000
4. Florida (C)	10.7%	15,000
5. Alabama (C)	10.4%	100,000
6. Tennessee (C)	10.4%	115,000
7. Arkansas (C)	10.4%	45,000
8. Virginia (C)	9.7%	155,000
9. Texas (C)	9.6%	58,000
10. South Carolina (C)	8.5%	60,000
11. Louisiana (C)	7.5%	53,000
12. Missouri (B)	3.4%	40,000
13. Maryland (B)	2.9%	20,000
14. Kentucky (B)	2.2%	25,000
15. Other (Indian Terr) (B)		5,000
Totals		**1,033,000**

Regional Summary

Border States	3.0%	90,000
Confederacy	10.4%	943,000

A "C" indicates a Confederate State, a "B" stands for a Border State.

The Confederate States by Proportion of White Population Enlisted in Confederate Service

State	% of White Population
1. Mississippi (C)	24.0%
2. Georgia (C)	22.0%
3. South Carolina (C)	20.6%
4. North Carolina (C)	20.2%

5. Florida (C)	19.3%
6. Alabama (C)	19.0%
7. Louisiana (C)	14.8%
8. Virginia (C)	14.8%
9. Arkansas (C)	13.9%
10. Tennessee (C)	13.9%
11. Texas (C)	13.8%
12. Maryland (B)	3.9%
13. Missouri (B)	3.8%
14. Kentucky (B)	2.7%
15. Other (Indian Terr) (B)	

Regional Summary

Border States	3.6%
Confederacy	17.3%

A "C" indicates a Confederate State, a "B" stands for a Border State.

Number of Confederate Troops Rejected after Physical Examination

Type of Troops	Number Rejected
Recruits 1864-1865	50,008 (22.1%)
Substitutes 1864-1865	21,125 (26.4%)
Conscripts 1863-1865	155,730 (25.7%)

Numbers Recruited for Union Service

The States and Territories Ranked by Manpower Recruited for the Union

State	Credited	% of Army	% of State Population
1. New York	448,850	16.0%	11.6%
2. Pennsylvania	337,936	12.1%	14.3%
3. Ohio	313,180	11.2%	13.4%
4. Illinois	259,092	9.2%	15.1%
5. Indiana	196,363	7.0%	14.5%
6. Massachusetts	146,730	5.2%	11.9%
7. Missouri (B)	109,111	3.9%	9.2%
8. Wisconsin	91,194	3.3%	11.8%
9. Michigan	87,364	3.1%	11.8%
10. New Jersey	76,814	2.7%	11.4%
11. Iowa	76,242	2.7%	11.3%
12. Kentucky (B)	75,760	2.7%	6.6%
13. Maine	70,107	2.5%	11.2%
14. Connecticut	55,864	2.0%	12.1%
15. Tennessee (C)	51,227	1.8%	4.6%
16. Maryland (B)	46,638	1.7%	6.8%
17. Virginia (C)	37,924	1.4%	2.4%
18. New Hampshire	33,937	1.2%	10.4%
19. Vermont	33,288	1.2%	10.6%
20. Louisiana (C)	29,276	1.0%	4.1%
21. Minnesota	24,020	0.9%	14.2%
22. Rhode Island	23,236	0.8%	13.3%
23. Kansas	20,149	0.7%	18.8%
24. Mississippi (C)	18,414	0.7%	2.3%

25. District of Columbia	16,534	0.6%	22.0%
26. California	15,725	0.6%	4.8%
27. Arkansas (C)	13,815	0.5%	3.2%
28. Delaware	12,284	0.4%	10.9%
29. North Carolina (C)	8,191	0.3%	0.8%
30. Alabama (C)	7,547	0.3%	0.8%
31. New Mexico Territory	6,561	0.2%	7.9%
32. South Carolina (C)	5,462	0.2%	0.8%
33. Colorado Territory	4,998	0.2%	14.6%
34. Indian Territory	3,530	0.1%	4.7%
35. Georgia (C)	3,486	0.1%	0.3%
36. Nebraska	3,157	0.1%	11.0%
37. Florida (C)	2,334	0.1%	1.7%
38. Texas (C)	2,012	0.1%	0.3%
39. Oregon	1,810	0.1%	3.5%
40. Nevada Territory	1,080	0.0%	15.8%
41. Washington Territory	964	0.0%	8.6%
42. Dakota Territory	206	0.0%	8.0%
43. Utah Territory	100	0.0%	0.2%
Total	**2,803,292**	**9.1%**	

"Credited" refers to the number of men which the state was credited with supplying to the Union. This includes men enlisted by the state who were not necessarily residents, such as most of the men credited to California, and also includes multiple enlistments, men who were discharged and later re-enlisted. As a result, the actual number of individuals who served is not known.

A "C" indicates a Confederate State, a "B" stands for a Border State.

States and Territories Ranked by Proportion of Population in Union Service

State	% of Population	Number Credited
1. District of Columbia	22.0%	16,534
2. Kansas	18.8%	20,149
3. Nevada Territory	15.8%	1,080
4. Illinois	15.1%	259,092

5. Colorado Territory	14.6%	4,998
6. Indiana	14.5%	196,363
7. Pennsylvania	14.3%	337,936
8. Minnesota	14.2%	24,020
9. Ohio	13.4%	313,180
10. Rhode Island	13.3%	23,236
11. Connecticut	12.1%	55,864
12. Massachusetts	11.9%	146,730
13. Wisconsin	11.8%	91,194
14. Michigan	11.8%	87,364
15. New York	11.6%	448,850
16. New Jersey	11.4%	76,814
17. Iowa	11.3%	76,242
18. Maine	11.2%	70,107
19. Nebraska	11.0%	3,157
20. Delaware	10.9%	12,284
21. Vermont	10.6%	33,288
22. New Hampshire	10.4%	33,937
23. Missouri (B)	9.2%	109,111
U.S. Average	**9.1%**	
24. Washington Territory	8.6%	964
25. Dakota Territory	8.0%	206
26. New Mexico Territory	7.9%	6,561
27. Maryland (B)	6.8%	46,638
28. Kentucky (B)	6.6%	75,760
29. California	4.8%	15,725
30. Indian Territory	4.7%	3,530
31. Tennessee (C)	4.6%	51,227
32. Louisiana (C)	4.1%	29,276
33. Oregon	3.5%	1,810
34. Arkansas (C)	3.2%	13,815
35. Virginia (C)	2.4%	37,924
36. Mississippi (C)	2.3%	18,414
37. Florida (C)	1.7%	2,334
38. North Carolina (C)	0.8%	8,191
39. Alabama (C)	0.8%	7,547

40. South Carolina (C)	0.8%	5,462
41. Texas (C)	0.3%	2,012
42. Georgia (C)	0.3%	3,486
43. Utah Territory	0.2%	100
Total		**2,803,292**

A "C" indicates a Confederate State, a "B" stands for a Border State.

The States and Territories Ranked by White Troops Furnished to the Union

State	Number of Troops	% of White Population
1. New York	409,561	10.7%
2. Pennsylvania	315,017	13.7%
3. Ohio	304,814	13.2%
4. Illinois	255,057	15.0%
5. Indiana	193,748	14.5%
6. Massachusetts	122,781	10.1%
7. Missouri	100,616	9.5%
8. Wisconsin	91,029	11.8%
9. Michigan	85,479	11.6%
10. Iowa	75,797	11.2%
11. New Jersey	67,500	10.4%
12. Maine	64,973	10.4%
13. Connecticut	51,937	11.5%
14. Kentucky (B)	51,743	5.6%
15. Maryland (B)	33,995	6.6%
16. New Hampshire	32,930	10.1%
17. Vermont	32,549	10.4%
18. Virginia (C)	31,872	3.0%
19. Tennessee (C)	31,092	3.8%
20. Minnesota	23,913	14.1%
21. Rhode Island	19,521	11.4%
22. Kansas	18,069	17.0%
23. California	15,725	4.9%
24. District of Columbia	11,912	19.6%

25. Delaware	11,236	12.4%
26. Arkansas (C)	8,289	2.6%
27. New Mexico Territory	6,561	7.9%
28. Louisiana (C)	5,224	1.5%
29. Colorado Territory	4,903	14.3%
30. Indian Territory	3,530	4.7%
31. Nebraska	3,157	11.0%
32. North Carolina (C)	3,156	0.5%
33. Alabama (C)	2,578	0.5%
34. Texas (C)	1,965	0.5%
35. Oregon	1,810	3.5%
36. Florida (C)	1,290	1.7%
37. Nevada Territory	1,080	15.9%
38. Washington Territory	964	8.7%
39. Mississippi (C)	545	0.2%
40. Dakota Territory	206	8.0%
41. Utah Territory	100	0.2%
42. South Carolina (C)	0	0.0%
43. Georgia (C)	0	0.0%
Total	**2,514,288**	**9.5%**

A "C" indicates a Confederate State, a "B" stands for a Border State.

The States and Territories Ranked by Proportion of White Population Furnished for Union Service

State	% of Whites	Number Credited
1. District of Columbia	19.6%	11,912
2. Kansas	17.0%	18,069
3. Nevada Territory	15.9%	1,080
4. Illinois	15.0%	255,057
5. Indiana	14.5%	193,748
6. Colorado Territory	14.3%	4,903

7. Minnesota	14.1%	23,913
8. Pennsylvania	13.7%	315,017
9. Ohio	13.2%	304,814
10. Delaware	12.4%	11,236
11. Wisconsin	11.8%	91,029
12. Michigan	11.6%	85,479
13. Connecticut	11.5%	51,937
14. Rhode Island	11.4%	19,521
15. Iowa	11.2%	75,797
16. Nebraska	11.0%	3,157
17. New York	10.7%	409,561
18. New Jersey	10.4%	67,500
19. Maine	10.4%	64,973
20. Vermont	10.4%	32,549
21. New Hampshire	10.1%	32,930
22. Massachusetts	10.1%	122,781
23. Missouri (B)	9.5%	100,616
U.S. Average	**9.5%**	
24. Washington Territory	8.7%	964
25. Dakota Territory	8.0%	206
26. New Mexico Territory	7.9%	6,561
27. Maryland (B)	6.6%	33,995
28. Kentucky (B)	5.6%	51,743
29. California	4.9%	15,725
30. Indian Territory	4.7%	3,530
31. Tennessee (C)	3.8%	31,092
32. Oregon	3.5%	1,810
33. Virginia (C)	3.0%	31,872
34. Arkansas (C)	2.6%	8,289
35. Florida (C)	1.7%	1,290
36. Louisiana (C)	1.5%	5,224
37. North Carolina (C)	0.5%	3,156
38. Alabama (C)	0.5%	2,578
39. Texas (C)	0.5%	1,965
40. Utah Territory	0.2%	100
41. Mississippi (C)	0.2%	545

42. South Carolina (C)	0.0%	0
43. Georgia (C)	0.0%	0
Total		**2,514,288**

A "C" indicates a Confederate State, a "B" stands for a Border State.

The States and Territories Ranked by Black Troops Recruited for Union Service

State	Number	% of Black Recruited	% of Black Residents
1. Louisiana (C)	24,052	6.9%	3.4%
2. Kentucky (B)	23,703	10.0%	2.1%
3. Tennessee (C)	20,135	7.1%	1.8%
4. Mississippi (C)	17,869	4.1%	2.3%
5. Maryland (B)	8,718	5.1%	1.3%
6. Pennsylvania	8,612	15.1%	0.4%
7. Missouri (B)	8,344	7.0%	0.7%
8. Virginia (C)	5,919	1.1%	0.4%
9. At Large	5,896	3.3%	
10. Arkansas (C)	5,526	5.0%	1.3%
11. South Carolina (C)	5,462	1.3%	0.8%
12. Ohio	5,092	13.9%	0.2%
13. North Carolina (C)	5,035	1.4%	0.5%
14. Alabama (C)	4,969	1.1%	0.5%
15. New York	4,125	8.4%	0.1%
16. Massachusetts	3,966	41.3%	0.3%
17. Georgia (C)	3,486	0.7%	0.3%
18. District of Columbia	3,269	22.8%	4.4%
19. Kansas	2,080	331.7%	1.9%
20. Rhode Island	1,837	46.5%	1.1%
21. Illinois	1,811	23.7%	0.1%
22. Connecticut	1,764	20.4%	0.4%
23. Indiana	1,537	13.4%	0.1%
24. Michigan	1,387	20.4%	0.2%
25. New Jersey	1,185	4.7%	0.2%
26. Florida (C)	1,044	1.7%	0.7%

27. Delaware	954	4.4%	0.9%
28. Iowa	440	41.2%	0.1%
29. Wisconsin	165	14.1%	0.0%
30. New Hampshire	125	25.3%	0.0%
31. Vermont	120	16.9%	0.0%
32. Minnesota	104	40.2%	0.1%
33. Maine	104	7.8%	0.0%
34. Colorado Territory	95	206.5%	0.3%
35. Texas (C)	47	0.0%	0.0%
36. New Mexico Territory	0	0.0%	0.0%
37. Dakota Territory	0	0.0%	0.0%
38. Nevada Territory	0	0.0%	0.0%
39. Utah Territory	0	0.0%	0.0%
40. California	0	0.0%	0.0%
41. Oregon	0	0.0%	0.0%
42. Indian Territory	0	0.0%	0.0%
43. Washington Territory	0	0.0%	0.0%
44. Nebraska	0	0.0%	0.0%
Total	**178,977**	**4.0%**	**0.6%**

"At Large" represents personnel recruited without being credited to the quota of any state.

A "C" indicates a Confederate State, a "B" stands for a Border State.

The States and Territories Ranked by Proportion of Black Residents Recruited for Union Service

	% of Blacks Recruited	Number of Recruits
1. Kansas	331.7%	2,080
2. Colorado Territory	206.5%	95
3. Rhode Island	46.5%	1,837
4. Massachusetts	41.3%	3,966
5. Iowa	41.2%	440
6. Minnesota	40.2%	104
7. New Hampshire	25.3%	125

8. Illinois	23.7%	1,811
9. District of Columbia	22.8%	3,269
10. Connecticut	20.4%	1,764
11. Michigan	20.4%	1,387
12. Vermont	16.9%	120
13. Pennsylvania	15.1%	8,612
14. Wisconsin	14.1%	165
15. Ohio	13.9%	5,092
16. Indiana	13.4%	1,537
17. Kentucky (B)	10.0%	23,703
18. New York	8.4%	4,125
19. Maine	7.8%	104
20. Tennessee (C)	7.1%•	20,135
21. Missouri (B)	7.0%	8,344
22. Louisiana (C)	6.9%	24,052
23. Maryland (B)	5.1%	8,718
24. Arkansas (C)	5.0%	5,526
25. New Jersey	4.7%	1,185
26. Delaware	4.4%	954
27. Mississippi (C)	4.1%	17,869
U.S. Average	4.0%	
28. Florida (C)	1.7%	1,044
29. North Carolina (C)	1.4%	5,035
30. South Carolina (C)	1.3%	5,462
31. Alabama (C)	1.1%	4,969
32. Virginia (C)	1.1%	5,919
33. Georgia (C)	0.7%	3,486
34. Texas (C)	0.0%	47
35. New Mexico Territory	0.0%	0
36. California	0.0%	0
37. Oregon	0.0%	0
38. Dakota Territory	0.0%	0
39. Indian Territory	0.0%	0
40. Utah Territory	0.0%	0
41. Nevada Territory	0.0%	0
42. Nebraska	0.0%	0

43. Washington Territory   0.0%   0
44. At Large   5,896
Total   **178,977**

The oddly disproportionate number of Black troops credited to some Northern and Western states was the result of those states recruiting among freedmen in the South and among Blacks at large, as in the case of the *54th Massachusetts Infantry*, which included men from all over the country.

A "C" indicates a Confederate State, a "B" stands for a Border State.

Summary of Union Enrollments

Command	Number of troops
Volunteers	2,080,193
Regulars	67,000
Colored Troops	178,975
Total	**2,326,168**

Strength of the Union Army

Strength of All Union Armies on Selected Dates

Date	Strength
1 January 1861	16,367
1 July 1861	186,751
1 January 1861	575,917
31 March 1862	637,126
1 January 1863	918,191
1 January 1864	860,737
31 March 1865	980,086
1 May 1865	1,000,516

Strength of the U.S. Regular Army on Selected Dates

Date	Strength
1 January 1861	16,267
1 July 1861	16,422
1 January 1862	22,425
31 March 1862	23,308
1 January 1863	25,463
1 January 1864	24,636
1 January 1865	22,019
31 March 1865	21,669

Portrait of the Union Army

Occupations of Union Soldiers

Occupation	% of Troops
Farmers	48%
Mechanics	24%
Laborers	16%
Commercial	5%
Professional	3%
Miscellaneous	4%

Average Height and Weight of Union Soldiers

Height Average: 5 feet, 8 1/4 inches
Weight Average: 143 1/2 pounds

Heights of Union Soldiers

Average Height: 5 feet, 8 1/4 inches
Tallest: Captain Van Buskirk, *27th Indiana*, 6 feet, 10 1/2 inches
Shortest: A private in the *192nd Ohio*, 3 feet, 4 inches

Hair Color of Union Soldiers

Hair Color	% of Troops
Brown	30%
Dark	25%
Light	24%
Black	13%
Sandy	4%
Red	3%
Gray	1%

Eye Color of Union Soldiers

Eye Color	% of Troops
Blue	45%
Gray	24%
Hazel	13%
Dark	10%
Black	8%

Complexion of Union Soldiers

Complexion	% of Troops
Light	60%
Dark	33%
Medium	7%

These figures probably do not include Black troops.

Height of Indiana Soldiers

Height	Number of Troops
Under 5 feet, 1 inch	501
5 feet, 1 inch	263
5 feet, 2 inches	971
5 feet, 3 inches	2,503
5 feet, 4 inches	5,387
5 feet, 5 inches	9,171
5 feet, 6 inches	14,373
5 feet, 7 inches	15,328
5 feet, 8 inches	19,140
5 feet, 9 inches	15,472
5 feet, 10 inches	15,047
5 feet, 11 inches	8,706
6 feet	6,679
6 feet, 1 inch	2,614
6 feet, 2 inches	1,357
6 feet, 3 inches	406
Over 6 feet, 3 inches	336
Total	**118,254**

Age of Indiana Soldiers at Enlistment

Age	Number of Troops
under 17	270
17	634
18	21,935
19	10,519
20	9,435
21	9,705
22	7,835
23	6,789
24	6,013
25	4,891
26	4,283

27	3,758
28	3,929
29	2,769
30	3,001
31-34	8,361
Over 34	14,127

Ethnic Composition of the Armies

American Indian Units to Serve with the Army of the Potomac

40th New York Infantry (Co. I)
53rd New York Infantry (1 Co.)

Nationalities of 179 Foreign-Born Lieutenants in the Confederate Army

Nationality	Lieutenants
Irish	63
German	59
French	8
Mexican	5
English	4
Canadian	3
Scottish	3
West Indies	2
Welsh	1
Spanish	1

Greek	1
Danish	1
Hungarian	1

Confederate Regiments of Foreign Born

Alabama

12th Infantry: 2 Companies (Co. A, French; Co. C, German)

21st Infantry: 2 Companies (Co. H, French, Co. K, mixed)

24th Infantry: 1 Company (Co. B, Irish)

Georgia

Frazier's Battery (Irish)

19th Infantry: 1 Company (Co. B, Irish)

21st Infantry: 1 Company (Co. E, German)

Louisiana

Avegno Zouaves (mixed)

1st Infantry: 3 Companies (Co. D, Irish; Co. E, Irish; Co. F., mixed)

5th Infantry: 3 Companies (Co. B, mixed; Co. C, Irish; Co. G, mixed)

6th Infantry: 6 Companies (Co. B, Irish; Co. G, German; Co. H, mixed; Co. K, mixed; Co. F, Irish; Co I, Irish)

7th Infantry: 2 Companies (Co. D, Irish; Co. F, Irish)

8th Infantry: 2 Companies (Co. B, mixed; Co. D, mixed)

9th Infantry: 1 Company (Co. E, Irish)

10th Infantry: 6 Companies (Irish and mixed)

14th Infantry: 6 Companies (Irish and mixed)

15th Infantry: 2 Companies (Co. B, mixed; Co. D, mixed)

20th Infantry: 6 Companies (German)

20th Infantry: 4 Companies (Irish)

Wheat's Battalion (Irish)

Garibaldi Legion: 1 Company (Italian)

Coppen's Zouaves: (mixed)

Note: For "Polish Brigade" see 14th and 15th Infantry (mixed). The "Defense Guards, European Brigade" had Australian, British, French, German, Italian and Spanish components.

North Carolina
7th Infantry: 1 Company (Co. D, mixed)
18th Infantry: 1 Company (Co. A, German)
40th Infantry: (Co. H, Irish)

South Carolina
Charleston Battalion (Irish and German)
Bachman's Battery (German)
Battery A, Light Artillery (German)
Battery B, Light Artillery (German)

Tennessee
2nd Infantry (Irish)
10th Infantry (Irish)
15th Infantry (Co. I, mixed)
21st Infantry (Co. B, Irish)

Texas
1st Heavy Artillery: 1 Company (Co. F, Irish)
1st Cavalry: 1 Company (Co. E, German)
2nd Cavalry: 1 Company (Co. F, German)
3rd Cavalry (7 Cos. German; 6 Cos. Mexican)
4th Cavalry: (Co. C, German)
5th Cavalry: (Co. E, German)
8th Cavalry: (Co. F, German)
Galveston "Davis" Artillery (German)
Turnverein Artillery (German)
Waul's Legion: 5 Companies (German)
8th Infantry: (Co. B, German; Co. C, Mexican)

Note: The "Home Guards" had numerous Mexican and German companies and one Polish company.

Virginia
Pelham's Horse Artillery (mixed)
Rains Artillery: Part (German)
Virginia Foreign Legion (British)
11th Infantry: 1 Company (Co. H, Irish)
17th Infantry: (Co. G, Irish; Co. I, Irish)

Number of Foreign Born Troops in the Union Army

Nationality	Number of Troops
German	175,000
Irish	150,000
English	50,000
Canadian	50,000
Other	75,000
Total	**500,000**

Union Regiments of Foreign Born

Dutch

2nd Michigan Cavalry (Co. D)

French

55th New York Infantry ("Guardes Lafayettes;" some members transferred to the 38th and 40th New York Infantry) 62nd New York Infantry (1 Co.)

German

1st Connecticut Infantry (Co. B)

6th Connecticut Infantry (Cos. B, H)

11th Connecticut (1 Co.)

Battery E, 2nd Illinois Artillery (half)

12th Illinois Cavalry (Co. B)

13th Illinois Cavalry (half)

9th Illinois Infantry (half)

24th Illinois Infantry (most)

27th Illinois Infantry (half)

36th Illinois Infantry (half)

43rd Illinois Infantry

44th Illinois Infantry (half)

45th Illinois Infantry (half)

57th Illinois Infantry (half)

58th Illinois Infantry (half)

82nd Illinois Infantry

1st Indiana Battery
6th Indiana Battery
14th Indiana Infantry (half)
24th Indiana Infantry (half)
32nd Indiana Infantry
136th Indiana Infantry (half)
1st Iowa Infantry (part)
16th Iowa Infantry (part)
1st Kansas Infantry (1 Co.)
2nd Kansas Infantry (half)
Battery A, 1st Kentucky Artillery (part)
2nd Kentucky Cavalry (part)
5th Kentucky Infantry (half)
6th Kentucky Infantry (half)
17th Massachusetts Infantry (1 Co.)
29th Massachusetts Infantry (1 Co.)
1st Minnesota Battery
1st Minnesota Infantry (one-third)
2nd Minnesota Infantry (one-third)
4th Minnesota Infantry (one-third)
6th Minnesota Infantry (one-third)
Battery B, 1st Missouri Artillery
Battery C, 1st Missouri Artillery
Essig's Battery, Missouri
Landgraber's Battery, Missouri
Mann's Battery, Missouri
Newstadter's Battery, Missouri
Wolfe's Battery, Missouri
1st Missouri Cavalry (Co. A)
4th Missouri Cavalry (most)
1st Missouri Infantry (half)
2nd Missouri Infantry
3rd Missouri Infantry
4th Missouri Infantry
5th Missouri Infantry
7th Missouri Infantry (Co. I)
12th Missouri Infantry

17th Missouri Infantry
18th Missouri Infantry (Co. K)
39th Missouri Infantry (half)
40th Missouri Infantry (half)
41st Missouri Infantry (half)
Missouri Home Guard (Five Regiments)
1st Veteran Nebraska Cavalry (half)
Battery A, New Jersey Artillery
Battery B, New Jersey Artillery (most)
Battery C, New Jersey Artillery (most)
3rd New Jersey Cavalry
Brick's Battery, 1st New York Battalion Light Artillery
15th New York Heavy Artillery
2nd New York Independent Battery
13th New York Independent Battery
Battery I, First New York Light Artillery
1st New York Cavalry (4 Cos.)
4th New York Cavalry (part)
5th New York Militia
7th New York Militia ("Steuben Rifles")
8th New York Infantry ("First German Rifles")
20th New York Infantry ("United Turner Regiment")
29th New York Infantry ("Astor Rifles")
39th N.Y. Garibaldi Guard (3 Cos.)
40th New York Infantry (Co. H)
41st New York Infantry ("Dekalb Regiment")
45th New York Infantry ("German Rifles No. 5")
46th New York Infantry ("Frement Regiment")
52nd New York Infantry ("Sigel Rifles")
54th New York Infantry (Schwarze Jager)
58th New York Infantry (part)
68th New York Infantry (part)
103rd New York Infantry ("German Rifles No. 3")
119 New York Infantry (one-third)
149th New York Infantry (part)
190th New York Infantry (part)
Battery I, 1st Ohio Light Artillery

4th Ohio Battery
8th Ohio Battery
20th Ohio Battery
3rd Ohio Cavalry (part)
9th Ohio Infantry
28th Ohio Infantry
37th Ohio Infantry
47th Ohio Infantry (half)
58th Ohio Infantry (half)
74th Ohio Infantry (half)
106th Ohio Infantry
107th Ohio Infantry
108th Ohio Infantry
165th Ohio Infantry
27th Pennsylvania Infantry
73rd Pennsylvania Infantry
75th Pennsylvania Infantry
98th Pennsylvania Infantry
1st Texas Infantry (most)
Battery E, 1st West Virginia Artillery

Irish

9th Connecticut Infantry
Battery L, 1st Illinois Infantry
19th Illinois Infantry
23rd Illinois Infantry
35th Indiana Infantry
61st Indiana Infantry
9th Massachusetts Infantry
15th Massachusetts Infantry
19th Massachusetts Infantry (Co. E)
28th Massachusetts Infantry
24th Michigan Infantry (part)
7th Missouri Infantry
10th New Hampshire Infantry (part)
14th New York Battery
15th New York Battery

11th New York Infantry (most)
37th New York Infantry
40th New York Infantry (Co. K)
63rd New York Infantry
69th New York Militia
69th New York Infantry
79th New York Infantry (part)
88th New York Infantry
105th New York Infantry (Cos. G, H, I)
155th New York Infantry
164th New York Infantry
170th New York Infantry
175th New York Infantry
182nd New York Infantry
8th Ohio Infantry (Co. B)
10th Ohio Infantry
61st Ohio Infantry (2 Cos.)
13th Pennsylvania Cavalry (part)
2nd Pennsylvania Reserves (Co. C)
13th Pennsylvania Reserves (Co. F)
24th Pennsylvania Reserves
69th Pennsylvania Reserves
106th Pennsylvania Reserves (part)
13th Vermont Infantry (Co. A)

Mexican

5 militia companies and one cavalry regiment in New Mexico
and Texas

Scandinavian

15th Wisconsin Infantry (Swedes)
3rd Wisconsin Infantry (Co. K, Danish)
3rd Minnesota (Co. D, mixed)
Battery H, 1st Illinois Artillery (mixed)
Battery G, 2nd Illinois Artillery (mixed)
33rd Illinois Infantry (Cos. E and G, Swedes)
36th Illinois Infantry (Co. F, Norwegian)
43rd Illinois Infantry (Cos. C and E, Swedes)

Scottish
79th New York Infantry (most)

Swiss
82nd Illinois Infantry (1 Co.)
15th Missouri Infantry (1 Co.)
9th New York Militia (1 Co.)
1st U.S. Sharpshooters (Co. G)

Welsh
97th New York (Co. E)

Mixed Nationalities
Enfants Perdus
89th Illinois (Co. D)
1st New York Cavalry (Co. E)
31st New York Infantry (some Polish)
39th New York ("Garibaldi Guard")
53rd New York Infantry (D'Epineuil Zouaves)
58th New York Infantry ("Polish Legion")
97 New York Infantry (Co. H)

The Two Most Polyglot Outfits in the War

1. The Confederate 1st Louisiana allegedly had men of 37 different nationalities in its ranks.
2. The Union *39th New York* (*Garibaldi Guard*) had men of fifteen different nationalities, so that seven languages were in common use: English, French, Italian, German, Hungarian, Spanish, and Portuguese.

Number of Jewish Soldiers

Army	Number of Jewish Troops
Union Army	6,000 - 8,500
Confederate Army	1,800 - 2,000

Unusual Units

Ten Union Regiments with Unusual Nicknames

1-3. The *13th Pennsylvania Reserves* (alternately the *1st Pennsylvania Rifles* or the *42nd Pennsylvania Volunteers*) was popularly known as the "Pennsylvania Bucktails." It was recruited from the lumbermen and backwoodsmen of the state, who had to demonstrate their marksmanship by producing a bucktail, which they usually fastened to their hats. Later the *149th* and *150th Pennsylvania* were recruited under much the same conditions, and were also called "Bucktails."

4-5. The *33rd Illinois* and the *151st Pennsylvania* were each known as "The Teachers' Regiment" because of the large number of teachers and students who were enrolled.

6. The *37th Iowa*, recruited for internal security and prisoner-of-war duty, was known as the "Graybeard Regiment" because it was composed entirely of men over 45 years of age: the average age was 57, and a few men were up in their 80s.

7. The *61st Pennsylvania* was known as "The California Regiment" because, although recruited in Pennsylvania, it was paid for by California.

8. The *89th Illinois* was known as "The Railroad Regiment" because it was recruited largely from railroad employees.

9. The *100th Indiana* was known as "The Persimmon Regiment," because the troops were wont to break ranks and gather the fruit whenever a persimmon tree was encountered.

10. The *118th Pennsylvania* was known as "The Corn Exchange Regiment" because it was recruited by, and to a great extent from the employees of, the Philadelphia Corn Exchange.

Fifteen Unusual Regiments
from New York State

1. *10th New York Infantry*, a zouave outfit, had so many Masons in it's ranks that it organized the "National Zouave Lodge," and often held regular meetings, even when in the field, to which fellow-Masons of the Confederate persuasion were welcome, if they happened to be around as prisoners-of-war.
2. *39th New York* (*Garibaldi Guard*) included men of fifteen different nationalities, so that seven languages were in common use: English, French, Italian, German, Hungarian, Spanish, and Portuguese.
3. *40th New York* ("*The Mozart Regiment*") was composed mostly of musicians. Four companies were from Massachusetts.
4. *42nd New York* ("*The Tammany Regiment*") was recruited from among the party stalwarts, and has the most distinctive monument at Gettysburg, an Indian tepee.
5. *46th New York* ("*The German Regiment*") was mostly composed of German emigre residents of the city.
6. *48th New York* ("*Perry's Saints*"), which was largely officered by clergymen.
7. *53rd New York* ("*The d'Epineuil Zouaves*"), a three-year regiment recruited in August of 1862 was so full of goldbricks, drunks, brawlers, and rowdies that it was mustered out of the service only seven months later.
8. 55th New York ("*The Lafayette Guards*") was composed of volunteers from the city's French *emigre* community.
9. *79th New York* "*Highlanders*" was composed principally of persons of Scottish descent, and actually wore the Cameron kilt—in honor of Secretary of War Simon Cameron, whose brother James commanded them—for a time, although never, apparently, in combat.
10-15. *131st, 133rd, 161st, 173rd,* and *174th New York Infantry* and the *14th New York Cavalry* were all recruited through the good offices of the New York City Metropolitan Police.

Weapons

Infantry Weapons of the Civil War

1. U.S. 1835 Musket

Muzzleloader; Caliber, .69; Range, 150 yards; Weight, 11.0 pounds
An antiquated weapon by the time of the Civil War, this gun was the last flintlock to be issued by the U.S. Army and was used by many troops early on in the conflict.

2. U.S. 1842 Musket

Muzzleloader; Caliber, .69; Range, 150 yards; Weight, 11.0 pounds
This gun was a modification of the 1835 flintlock musket. The new version included a percussion cap along with other changes. It fired ball ammunition, buck and ball and even buckshot. This dated weapon was still being used by 1863, but was disappearing in favor of more effective modern weapons.

3. U.S. 1855 Rifle

Muzzleloader; Caliber, .58; Range, 400 yards; Weight, 10.1 pounds
The first minie rifle issued to U.S. troops. Some 100,000 were produced before the war.

4. U.S. 1861 Rifle

Muzzleloader; Caliber, .58; Range, 450 yards; Weight, 9.75 pounds
This weapon, called the Springfield rifle, saw the widest use in the war. Around 1,500,000 were produced, some of which found their way to Confederate ranks primarily through capture. The 1861 version was the primary type issued during the war, but two other types were produced.

5. Sharps 1848 Carbine

Breechloader; Caliber, .52; Range, 350 yards; Weight, 7.0 pounds
A popular cavalry weapon, the Sharps carbine was the first breech loading firearm to be issued to U.S. troops.

6. Sharps 1848 Rifle

Breechloader; Caliber, .52; Range, 450 yards; Weight, 8.0 pounds
A breech loading rifle designed by Christian Sharps. A comparatively small number of these guns were produced and primarily were issued to special units, like the elite *Berdan's Sharpshooters*.

7. Spencer 1860 Carbine

Breech Loader; Caliber, .52; Range, 450 yards; Weight, 8.3 pounds
Christopher M. Spencer's carbine, patented in 1860, was the first regularly issued repeating firearm in the world. The gun had a tubular magazine for seven copper cased, rim fire cartridges which was inserted in the stock of the weapon. Around 200,000 Spencer carbines were issued during the war.

8. Enfield 1855 Rifle.

Muzzle Loader, Caliber, .577; Range, 350 yards, Weight, 8.0 pounds
These well built and serviceable weapons from Great Britain saw active use in the war on both sides. Some 500,000 were purchased during the war by the Union. The South managed to get around 100,000 of these guns.

Six Weapons Used for the First Time in the Civil War

1. The Machinegun: Five different machine guns were used during the war, mostly in the early period. The most successful of these were the Union's Ager Repeating Gun, and the Confederacy's Williams Rapid-Fire Gun, which was actually a rapid fire very light artillery piece. Although the Gatling Gun came along late in the war, it's use was very limited. Although these were all rather promising devices, there were numerous technical and bureaucratic obstacles to the more extensive use of such weapons, and they had little impact on the war.

2. The Landmine: Confederate Brig. Gen. Gabriel J. Rains, an ordnance expert, developed the first genuine anti-personnel contact mines in early 1862. Large numbers of these were used during the opening stages of the Peninsula Campaign that Spring to impede the Union advance on Richmond. Despite some success, the devices were rather difficult to produce and were considered rather dishonorable, not alone by Union personnel. As a result, they say only limited use in the war.

3. The Observation Balloon: Both sides experimented with the use of balloons to observe the activities of the enemy from the air, map terrain and spot for artillery. The South with its limited resources only managed to make a few ascents. The Union had a U.S. Balloon Corps headed by

aeronaut Thaddeus Lowe which was active early in the war, but was disbanded in 1863.

4. The Anti-Aircraft Gun: a 3" Rifle which Union Capt. Thomas W. Osborn of *D Battery, 1st New York Light Artillery* rigged for high angle fire was used several times during the Peninsula campaign, none of which succeeded in bringing down a Confederate balloon.

5. The Repeating Rifle: Although most of the perhaps five million shoulder arms procured during the Civil War (about four million by the Union and a further million or so by the Confederacy, not counting captures), were single shot muzzle loaders, about 400,000 breech loading repeating rifles and carbines were also issued, in more than a dozen different makes and models, most notably the Spencer Repeating Carbine, of which about 100,000 were used by the Union, and the Sharps Carbine, of which about 80,000 were issued by the Union. Although some of the less widely issued repeating firearms were not successful, both the Spencer and the Sharps were excellent weapons which rendered good service. Were it not for bureaucratic opposition on the part of Union ordnance officers all Federal troops could have been issued such weapons by the end of the war.

6. The Mounted Railroad Cannon: Given the importance of railroads during the Civil War, it was only natural that weapons find their place on trains. The most famous rail mounted gun was the *Dictator*, a 13-inch mortar which sat on a flatcar.

CHAPTER 2

BATTLES

Campaigns, Battles and Special Actions

Civil War Campaigns

Antietam Campaign, 4-22 Sept. 1862

Appomattox Campaign, 25 Mar.-9 Apr. 1865

Atlanta Campaign, 1 May-2 Sept. 1864

Bull Run Campaign, First, 16-22 Jly. 1861; Second, 26 Aug.-1 Sept. 1862

Bristoe Campaign, 9-22 Oct. 1863

Chancellorsville Campaign, 27 Apr.-6 May 1863

Chattanooga Campaign, 1 Oct.-25 Nov. 1863

Chickamauga Campaign, 16 Aug.-23 Sept. 1863

Early's Washington Raid, 23 June-12 Jly. 1864

Fort Henry and Fort Donelson Campaigns, 6-16 Feb. 1862

Franklin and Nashville Campaigns, 29 Nov.-27 Dec. 1864

Fredericksburg Campaign, 15 Nov.-15 Dec. 1862

Gettysburg Campaign, 3 June-14 Jly. 1863

Grant's Overland Campaign, 4 May-12 June 1864

Jackson's Shenandoah Valley Campaign, 23 Feb.-9 June 1862

Knoxville Campaign, 4 Nov.-15 Dec. 1863

March to the Sea, 15 Nov.-10 Dec. 1864

Meridian Campaign, 3 Feb.-4 Mar. 1864

Mine Run Campaign, 26 Nov.-2 Dec. 1863

Peninsula Campaign, 17 Mar.-2 Aug. 1862

Perryville Campaign, 14 Aug.-26 Oct. 1862

Petersburg Campaign, 15 June 1864-3 Apr. 1865

Red River Campaign, 11 Mar.-20 May 1864

Seven Days Campaign, 25 June-1 Jly. 1862

Sheridan's Shenandoah Valley Campaign, 7 Aug. 1864-2 Mar. 1865

Sherman's Carolina Campaign, 1 Feb.-Apr. 26 1865

Sibley's New Mexico Campaign, Nov. 1861-4 May 1862

Spotsylvania Campaign, 7-19 May 1864

Tullahoma Campaign, 23 June-3 Jly. 1863

Vicksburg Campaign, First 16 Oct.-20 Dec. 1862; Second 1 Apr.-4 Jly. 1862

Prominent Land Battles, Engagements and Skirmishes of the Civil War

Aldie, VA, 17 June 1863

Allatoona, GA, 5 Oct. 1864

Allen's Farm, VA, 29 June 1862

Antietam, MD, 17 Sept. 1862

Atlanta, GA, 22 Jly. 1864

Averasborough, N.C., 16 Mar. 1865

Champion's Hill, MS, 16 May 1863

Ball's Bluff (Conrad's Ferry, Harrison's Island, Leesburg), VA, 21 Oct. 1861

Baton Rouge, LA, 5 Aug. 1862

Bayou Bourbeau, LA, 3 Nov. 1863

Bayou La Fourche, LA, 13 Jly. 1863

Belmont, MO, 7 Nov. 1861

Bentonville, N.C., 19-21 Mar. 1865

Big Bethel (Bethel Church), VA, 10 June 1861

Big Black River Bridge, MS, 17 May 1863

Bird Creek (Chusto-Talasah, High Shoal) Indian Territory, 9 Dec. 1861

Birdsong Ferry, MS, 5 Jly. 1863

Blackburn's Ford, VA, 18 Jly. 1861

Blountsville, TN, 22 Sept. 1863

Blue Springs, TN, 5,7,10 Oct. 1863

Burgess' Mill (Boyden Plank Road), VA, 27 Oct. 1864

Brandy Station, VA, 9 June 1863

Brice's Cross Roads (Guntown, Tishomingo Creek), MS, 10 June 1864

Bristoe Station, VA, 14 Oct. 1863

Buck Head Creek, GA, 28 Nov. 1864

Buckland Mills, VA, 19 Oct. 1863

Bull Run (Manassas), VA, First, 21 Jly. 1861; Second, 29-30 Aug. 1862

Burgess' Mill, VA, 27 Oct. 1864

Campbell's Station, TN, 16 Nov. 1863

Cane River Crossing, TN, 23 Apr. 1864

Carnifix Ferry, WV, 10 Sept. 1861

Carthage, MO, 5 Jly. 1861

Cedar Creek, VA, 19 Oct. 1864

Cedar Mountain, VA, 9 Aug. 1862

Chaffin's Farm, VA, 29-30 Sept. 1864

Champion Hill, MS, 16 May 1863

Chancellorsville, VA, 1-4 May 1863

Chantilly (Ox Hill), VA, 1 Sept. 1862

Chattanooga, TN, 23-25 Nov. 1863

Cheat Mountain, WV, 11-13 Sept. 1861

Chickamauga, GA, 19-20 Sept. 1863

Chickasaw Bluffs, MS, 27-29 Dec. 1862

Cloyd's Mountain, VA, 9 May 1864

Coffeeville, MS, 5 Dec. 1862

Corpus Christi, TX, 16-18 Aug. 1862

Cold Harbor, VA, 27 June 1862; 1-3 June 1864

Corinth, MS, 3-4 Oct. 1862

Corrick's Ford, WV, 13 Jly. 1861

Crampton's Gap, MD, 14 Sept. 1862

Crater, VA, 30 Jly. 1864

Cross Keys, VA, 8 June 1862

Dallas, GA, 28 May 1864

Darbytown (Deep Bottom, New Market Road, Strawberry Plains), VA, 27 Jly. 1864

Darbytown Road, VA, 7 and 27 Oct. 1864

Dinwiddie Court House, VA, 31 Mar. 1865

Dranesville, VA, 20 Dec. 1861

Drewry's Bluff (Fort Darling), VA, 16 May 1864

Droop Mountain, WV, 6 Nov. 1863

Ebenezer Church, VA, 1 Apr. 1865

Eltham's Landing (Barhamsville, West Point), VA, 7 Mar. 1862

Ezra Church, GA, 28 Jly. 1864

Fair Gardens (Kelly's Ford), TN, 27 Jan. 1864

Falling Waters, MD, 14 Jly. 1863

Fisher's Hill, VA, 22 Sept. 1864

Five Forks, VA, 1 Sept. 1865

Fort Bisland, VA, 14 Apr. 1863

Fort Brooke, FL, 16 Oct; 25 Dec. 1863

Fort Donelson, TN, 13-16 Feb. 1862

Fort Gregg, VA, 2 Apr. 1865

Fort Henry, TN, 6 Feb. 1862

Fort Pillow, TN, 12 Apr. 1864

Fort Sanders, TN, 29 Nov. 1863

Fort Stedman, VA, 25 Mar. 1865

Fort Sumter, S.C., 12 Apr. 1861

Franklin, TN, 30 Nov. 1864

Franklin's Crossing (Deep Run), VA, 5 June 1863

Fredericksburg Va, First Battle of, 13 Dec. 1862; Second Battle of, 3-4 May 1863

Front Royal, VA, 23 May 1862

Front Royal (Guard Hill), VA, 16 Aug. 1864

Gaines' Mill, VA, 27 June 1862

Galveston, TX, 1 Jan. 1863

Gettysburg, PA, 1-3 Jly. 1863

Glorietta Pass, New Mexico Territory, 26-28 Mar. 1862

Groveton (Brawner's Farm), VA, 28 Aug. 1862

Harper's Ferry, 13-15 Sept. 1862

Hatcher's Run (Armstrong's Mill; Boydton Plank Road; Dabney's Mill; Vaughan Road), VA, 5-7 Feb. 1865

Honey Hill, SC, 30 Nov. 1864

Honey Springs (Elk Creek), Indian Territory, 17 Jly. 1863

Irish Bend, 13 Apr. 1863

Island Number 10, MO, 7 Apr. 1862

Iuka, MS, 19 Sept. 1862

Ivy Mountain, KY, 8 Nov. 1861

Jackson, MS, 14 May 1863

Jonesborough, GA, 31 Aug.-1 Sept. 1864

Jug Tavern, GA, 3 Aug. 1864

Kelly's Ford, VA, 17 Mar. 1863

Kennesaw Mountain, GA, 27 June 1864

Kernstown, VA, First Battle of, 23 Mar. 1862; Second, VA, 24 Jly. 1864

Kinston, NC, 8-10 Mar. 1865

Lake Chicot (Ditch Bayou), AK, 6 June 1864

Laurel Hill, WV, 7 Jly. 1861

Leggett's Hill, GA, 21 Jly. 1862

Lexington, TN, 18 Dec. 1862

Lookout Mountain, TN, 24 Nov. 1863

Lynchburg, VA, 16-18 June 1864

McDowell, VA, 8 May 1862

Malvern Hill, VA, 1 Jly. 1862

Manassas Gap (Crew's Farm; Poindexter's Farm), VA, 22 Jly. 1863

Mansfield, LA (Pleasant Grove, Sabine's Crossroads, 8 Apr. 1864

Marais des Cygnes River, MO, 25 Oct. 1864

Mechanicsville (Beaver Dam Creek; Ellerson's Mill), VA, 26 June 1862

Middle Creek, KY, 10 Jan. 1862

Mill Springs (Beech Grove; Fishing Creek; Logan's Cross Roads; Somerset), KY, 19 Jan. 1862

Missionary Ridge, TN, 25 Nov. 1863

Monocacy, MD, 9 Jly. 1864

Monroe's Cross Roads, N.C., 10 Mar. 1865

Moorefield, WV, 7 Aug. 1864

Nashville, TN, 15-16 Dec. 1864

New Hope Church, GA, 23-27 May 1864

New Market Heights, 29 Sept. 1864

Newtonia, MO, First, 30 Sept. 1862; Second, 28 Oct. 1862

Norfleet House, VA, 14-15 Apr. 1863

North Anna River, VA, 23-26 May 1864

Oak Grove (French's Field; King's School House; The Orchard), VA, 25 June 1862

Okolana, MS, 22 Feb. 1864

Olustee, FL, 20 Feb. 1864

Orchard Knob, TN, 23 Nov. 1863

Paducah, KY, 25 Mar. 1864

Palmito Ranch, TX, 12-13 May 1865

Parker's Cross Roads, TN, 31 Dec. 1862

Pattersonville, LA, 28 Mar. 1863

Payne's Farm, VA, 27 Nov. 1863

Peachtree Creek, GA, 20 Jly. 1864

Pea Ridge (Elkhorn Tavern), AK, 7-8 Mar. 1862

Peebles' Farm, VA, 30 Sept.-2 Oct. 1864

Perryville (Chaplin Hills), KY, 8 Oct. 1862

Phillipi, WV, 3 June 1861

Pickett's Mill, GA, 27 May 1864

Piedmont, VA, 5 June 1864

Pleasant Hill, LA, 9 Apr. 1864

Plum Run Bend (Plum Point Bend), TN, 10 May 1862

Poison Springs, AK, 18 Apr. 1864

Port Gibson, MS, 1 May 1863

Port Republic, VA, 9 June 1862

Prairie Grove, AK, 7 Dec. 1862

Rappahannock Station, VA, 7 Nov. 1863

Raymond, MS, 12 May 1863

Reams Station, VA, 25 Aug. 1864

Resaca, GA, 14-15 May 1864

Richmond, KY, 29-30 Aug. 1862

Rich Mountain, WV, 11 Jly. 1861

Roanoke Island, NC, 8 Feb. 1862

Rocky Gap (White Sulphur Springs), WV, 26 Aug. 1863

Rocky Face Ridge, 7-9 May 1864

Sabine Pass, TX, 8 Sept. 1863

Salem Church (Salem Heights), VA, 3 May 1863

Salisbury, NC, 12 Apr. 1865

Savage's Station, VA, 29 June 1862

Shepherdstown, WV, 20 Sept. 1862

Sayler's Creek, VA, 6 Apr. 1865

Secessionville, SC, 16 June 1862

Seven Pines (Fair Oaks), VA, 31 May-1 June 1862

Shiloh (Pittsburg Landing), TN, 6-7 Apr.1862

South Mountain, MD, 14 Sept. 1862

Spring Hill, TN, 19 Nov. 1864

Stone's River (Murfreesboro), TN, 31 Dec. 1862-2 Jan. 1863

Sutherland's Station, VA, 2 Apr. 1865

Swift Creek, VA, 9 May 1864

Taylor's Ridge, GA, 27 Nov. 1863

Trevalian Station, VA, 11-12 June 1864

Tunnel Hill (Buzzard's Roost), GA, 24-25 Feb. 1864

Tupelo (Harrisburg), MS., 14-15 Jly. 1864

Valverde, New Mexico Territory, 21 Feb. 1862

Vining's Station, GA, 4 Jly. 1864

Waynesborough, GA, 4 Dec. 1864

Waynesborough, VA, 2 Mar. 1865

Westport, MO, 23 Oct. 1864

White Oak Road, VA, 31 Mar. 1865

White Oak Swamp (Charles City Crossroads, Frayser's Farm, Nelson's Cross Roads, New Market Road, Turkey Bridge, Willis Church), VA, 30 June 1862

Wilderness, VA, 5-7 May 1864

Williamsburg, VA, 5 May 1862

Wilmington, NC, 12-22 Feb. 1865

Wilson's Creek, MO, 10 Aug. 1861

Winchester (Oak Hills, Springfield), VA, First Battle of, 25 May 1862, Second Battle of, 14-15 June 1863, Third Battle of 19 Sept. 1864

Yellow Bayou (Bayou De Glaize, Norwood's Plantation, Old
   Oaks), LA, 18 May 1864
Yellow Tavern, VA, 11 May 1864

Ten Actions by Black Troops *Before* the Celebrated Attack of the *54th Massachusetts* on Fort Wagner on 18 July 1863

1. Island Mounds, MO, 29 Oct. 1862: *1st Kansas Colored Volunteers (79th U.S.C.I.)*.
2. Township, FL, 26 Jan. 1863: *1st South Carolina (33rd U.S.C.I.)*.
3. Baldwin, FL, 29 Mar. 1863: *1st South Carolina (33rd U.S.C.I.)*.
4. East Pascagoula, MS, 9 Apr. 1863: *2nd Louisiana Native Guards (74th U.S.C.I.)*.
5. Sherwood, MO, 18 May 1863: *1st Kansas Colored Volunteers (79th U.S.C.I.)*.
6. Lake Providence, LA, 27 May 1863: *47th U.S.C.I.*
7. Port Hudson, LA, 27 May-9 Jly. 1863: *1st* and *3rd Louisiana Native Guards (73rd* and *75th U.S.C.I.)*.
8. Milliken's Bend, LA, 6-8 June 1863: *5th U.S. Colored Heavy Artillery*, with the *9th* and *11th Louisiana Colored Volunteers (49th* and *51st U.S.C.I.)*.
9. Cabin Creek, Indian Territory, 1-2 Jly. 1863: *1st Kansas Colored Volunteers (79th U.S.C.I.)*.
10. Secessionville, SC, 16 Jly. 1863: *54th Massachusetts*.

Six Notable Fights Involving Indians

While the U.S. government was initially pressed by the emergency of secession to strip regular Western garrisons, various Indian outbreaks eventually resulted in large concentrations of troops stationed on the frontier—many state volunteers and Confederate prisoners who agreed to fight Indians as bluecoated "Galvanized Yankees." Besides employing Indian allies in frontier warfare, Yankees and Rebels also employed Indian regiments in fighting each other, especially those drawn from the so-called Five Civilized Tribes of the Indian Territory (later Oklahoma). While Indians were considered deficient in some non-combat aspects of soldiering, they enjoyed a generally high reputation as fighters.

1. Dove Creek, 9 Jan. 1865: Ignoring indications that an Indian band migrating through Texas was not hostile, Texas Confederate troops and state militiamen under Captain Henry Fossett rashly attacked a camp fortified by a surrounding thicket of live oak and briar. Stampeding the Indians' horse herds, the Texans were ambushed by better-armed foemen firing new Enfield rifles. The Indians were Kickapoos and a few Potawatomies who, tired of war after serving the Confederacy in Kansas, were headed toward Mexico. Despite the Kickapoos' relatively docile reputation, the Indians counterattacked, recovering most of their mounts and routing the Confederates in perhaps the most embarrassing White defeat in Texas Indian-fighting history. The White survivors, having lost at least 22 dead and over 60 wounded, retreated for four days, at times in hip deep snow, before reuniting with their cannibalistic Tonkawa Indian scouts and nourishing themselves on captured ponies which the Tonkawas had retained. The Kickapoos conceded only 14 dead.

2. Round Mountain, Indian Territory, 19 Nov. 1861: Texas cavalrymen and Confederate Indians under Colonel Douglas H. Cooper attempted to head off thousands of pro-Union and neutralist Indians, mostly Creeks under their leader Opothleyahala. After Confederate Cherokees had refused to fight the Creeks, some less squeamish Choctaws attempted to breech Creek defenses, allegedly slaughtering over a thousand warriors and noncombatants in the process. Though an attack by the Texas cavalrymen was repelled, the Creeks hastily fled by night without burying their slain. After several more defeats, the remaining refugees ultimately reached Kansas, many in a starving condition.

3. Pea Ridge or Elkhorn Tavern, Arkansas, 7-8 Mar. 1862: Confederate Maj. Gen. Earl Van Dorn, recipient of four wounds fighting Indians in the pre-war Army, enjoyed a rare numerical advantage when he attacked Federal forces astride the main road to southwestern Missouri. Van Dorn's force included an Indian brigade of Cherokees and Creeks under Brig. Gen. Albert Pike. Pike's brigade joined in the initial Rebel attack—but upon coming under

artillery fire, the Indians (later accused of scalping and other atrocities) took to the woods, potting away from behind trees with little effect. Retreating unbroken, the Federals counterattacked the next day and routed the Rebels. Cherokee leader Stand Watie would go on to become a brigadier—and the last Confederate general to surrender his command.

4. Sand Creek, Colorado, 29 Nov. 1864: U.S. Col. John M. Chivington, whose Colorado troops included his own cavalry regiment of 90-day militia volunteers, attacked a Cheyenne-Arapaho village of about 100 lodges under chiefs Black Kettle and White Antelope. Reporting casualties of 9 killed and 38 wounded, Chivington claimed 600 Indians, almost all warriors, slain: "All did nobly," he announced. But Congressional investigators condemned the incident after compiling evidence that the Indians had believed themselves under army protection and that Whites slaughtered women and children while savagely mutilating their bodies. Arapaho chief White Antelope's scrotum was supposedly cut off to use as a tobacco pouch. A fiery abolitionist preacher, Chivington had earlier served as Methodist missionary to Indians and formed a Masonic lodge with largely Indian membership. Unfortunately, the army found it could not court martial him, since he was not in Federal service.

5. Killdeer Mountain, North Dakota, 28 Jly. 1864: In a follow-up campaign to the 1862 Santee Sioux uprising in Minnesota—the bloodiest Indian massacre in U.S. history—General Alfred Sully pitted his 2,200 troops against an estimated 1,600 to 6,000 Teton Sioux warriors in the largest Indian fight seen on the Plains up to that time. Marching against the Indian camp, a huge square of dismounted cavalry and infantry enclosing artillery and horses, Sully repelled the most serious Sioux counterthrust with howitzer fire. Following up with a rare saber charge, he then bombarded the Indians rather than fight them in the timber to which they had fled. Losing 5 killed and 10 wounded and estimating 100 to 159 Sioux dead (the Indians conceding only 31), Sully was most pleased with the chance to capture and burn their village, wisely observing: "I would rather destroy their supplies than kill fifty of their warriors."

6. First Adobe Walls, Texas, 25 Nov. 1864: Brig. Gen. Christopher "Kit" Carson led a mixed cavalry and infantry force of slightly over 400 men—mostly New Mexico and California volunteers plus over 70 Ute and Apache warriors—in search of Comanche and Kiowas raiding along the Santa Fe Trail. He found them near the crumbling adobe ruins of an old trading post in the Texas Panhandle (where white buffalo hunters would be memorably besieged by Kiowas and Comanches in 1874). Fearing he had been discovered, Carson launched a hasty cavalry attack to seize a large Kiowa village under Little Mountain. But the Kiowas soon rallied, reinforced by Comanches from an even larger village, and Carson's men fought a desperate dismounted action near the old post before retreating—blasting the Kiowas from their reoccupied village with artillery shells and burning 176 tepees. But Carson had failed to destroy the Comanche village and escaped disaster largely thanks to what the Indians termed his "guns that shot twice"—two 12-pound mountain howitzers firing explosive shells.

The Six Most Daring "Special Operations" of the War

1. The Andrews Raid ("The Great Locomotive Chase"): Having infiltrated into the Confederacy on the night of 12 Apr. 1862, 21 Union volunteers under James J. Andrews, a civilian, stole the locomotive "The General" on the route from Marietta to Big Shanty, Georgia, and proceeded to rip up telegraph lines and inflict other damage on the route to Chattanooga. Pursued by trainloads of Confederate troops, the raiders managed to make about 90 miles before running out of fuel. Although they dispersed into the surrounding forest, all were captured. Andrews and seven others were later hanged. Of the remainder, eight escaped from captivity some months later and the balance were eventually paroled.

2. The Capture of Union Brig. Gen. Edwin H. Stoughton: On the night of 8 Mar. 1863 Confederate Capt. John S. Mosby and 29 of his men infiltrated Union lines and descended on Stoughton's headquarters at Fairfax Court House,

capturing the general in his nightshirt and carrying him off as a prisoner, along with 32 other men and some 58 horses.

3. The City Point Explosion: On 9 Aug. 1864 a Confederate agent planted an "horological torpedo' (*i.e.*, a time bomb) aboard an ammunition barge tied up at City Point, Virginia. The resulting explosion killed at least 43 and wounded 126, in addition to destroying two barges loaded with ammunition as well as a warehouse and a considerable portion of dock, for a loss of about $2,000,000.

4. The Lake Erie Operation: On 19 Sept. John Beall, a Confederate naval officer operating undercover in Canada, and a band of men seized the lake steamer *Philo Parsons* and set course for Sandusky, Ohio, with the intention of seizing the U.S. gunboat *Michigan*, the only Federal warship on the Great Lakes, and using her to liberate some 3,000 Confederate prisoners-of-war held at Johnson's Island. The idea was to stage a collision with the gunboat, and then board her in the confusion. However, this failed, and Beall had no choice but to abort the operation. Whilst steaming back to Canada, Beall managed to seize and scuttle the American steamer *Island Queen*, the only naval casualty of the war on the Great Lakes. Soon afterwards, Beall's ship ran aground on the Canadian side, but he and his men managed to elude capture.

5. The St. Albans Raid: In Oct. of 1864 Confederate Lt. Bennett H. Young and about 25 men infiltrated into Vermont from Canada in the guise of hunters. The group drifted into St. Albans over several days, and on 19 Oct. managed to seize the town, although not all of its inhabitants. While Young's men cleaned out the local banks and rounded up horses in anticipation of making a speedy escape, fugitives from the town alerted the local populace, who soon organized a posse. Outnumbered, Young and his men fled towards the border, breaking up into several groups in order to elude pursuit. About a dozen of the raiders were captured, but on Canadian soil, and the Canadian authorities ruled that the men had been acting as soldiers under orders and they were interned as such for the balance of the war.

6. The Attempt to Burn New York: In the autumn of 1864 Col. Robert M. Martin and seven other Confederate agents

gathered in New York City for the purpose of putting it to the torch by setting numerous fires in hotels on the night of 25 Nov. 1864. Although well supplied with incendiaries (some 402 vials), they proved unfamiliar with the city and inept arsonists. As a result, although some fires were set, the overall effect was minimal, the only significant damage being that to P.T. Barnum's Museum, which burned spectacularly and proved a total loss, including the Egress. Martin and his men managed to elude capture and made their way to Canada.

Battles With Multiple Names

One Battle With Seven Names

1. White Oak Swamp/Frayser's Farm/Glendale/Charles City Cross Roads/Nelson's Farm/Turkey Bend/New Market Cross Roads, VA, 30 June 1862.

Six Battles With Five Names

1. Bayou Cache/Cotton Plant/Round Hill/Bayou de View/Hill's Plantation, AK, 7 Jly. 1862
2. Cedar Mountain/Slaughter Mountain/Southwest Mountain/Cedar Run/Mitchell's Station, VA, 9 Aug. 1862
3. Irish Bend/Bisland/Bayou Teche/Indian Ridge/Centreville, LA, 12-14 Apr. 1863
4. Bayou de Glaize/Old Oaks/Yellow Bayou/Simmsport/Calhoun Station, LA, 18 May 1864
5. Dallas/New Hope Church/Burned Hickory/Pumpkin Vine Creek/Altoona Hills, GA, 25 May-4 June 1864
6. Kennesaw Mountain/Lost Mountain/Nose's Creek/Marietta/Big Shanty, GA, 9-30 June 1864

Four Battles with Four Names

1. West Glaze/Shanghai/Henrytown/Monday's Hollow, MO, 13 Oct. 1861
2. Ball's Bluff/Edward's Ferry/Harrison's Island/Leesburg, VA, 21 Oct. 1861
3. Champion Hill/Baker's Creek/Raymond/Bolton Depot, MS, 4 Feb. 1864
4. Mansura/Avoyelle's Prairie/Moreausville/Marksville, LA, 14-16 May 1864

Twelve Notable Battles with Two or Three Names

1. First Bull Run/First Manassas, VA, 21 Jly. 1861
2. Wilson's Creek/Springfield/Oak Hills, MO, 10 Aug. 1861
3. Fort Donelson/Dover, KY, 14-16 Feb. 1862
4. Pea Ridge/Bentonville/Elkhorn Tavern, AK, 5-8 Mar. 1862
5. Winchester/Kearnstown, VA, 23 Mar. 1862
6. Shiloh/Pittsburg Landing, TN, 6-7 Apr. 1862
7. Seven Pines/Fair Oaks, VA, 31 May-1 June 1862
8. Gaines' Mill/Cold Harbor/Chickahominy, VA, 27-28 June 1862
9. Second Bull Run/Manassas/Second Manassas, VA, 30 Aug. 1862
10. Chantilly/Oak Hill, VA, 1 Sept. 1862
11. Antietam/Sharpsburg, MD, 17 Sept. 1862
12. Champion Hills/Baker's Creek/Edward's Station, MS, 16 May 1863

Note: About 10 percent of the approximately 2,250 battles, skirmishes, and engagements of the Civil War have more than one name.

The Five Most Oddly Named Civil War Battles

1. Island Number Ten, MO, 7 Apr. 1862

2. Cumberland Iron Works, TN, 3 Feb. 1863
3. Duck River Shoals, TN, 24 Apr. 1863
4. Greasy Creek, KY, 11 May 1863
5. French Broad, TN, 27 Jan. 1864

Significant Battles

The Ten Best Commanded Battles of the War

1. Chancellorsville, VA, 1-4 May 1863 by C.S. Gen. Robert E. Lee
2. Second Manassas, VA, 29-30 Aug. 1862 by C.S. Gen. Robert E. Lee
3. Nashville, TN, 15-16 Dec. 1864 by U.S. Maj. Gen. George Thomas
4. Brice's Crossroads, MS, 10 June 1864 by C.S. Lt. Gen. Nathan Bedford Forrest
5. Cedar Creek, VA, 19 Oct. 1864 by U.S. Maj. Gen. Phil Sheridan
6. Shiloh, TN, 6-7 Apr. 1862 by U.S. Maj. Gen. Ulysses S. Grant
7. Franklin, TN, 30 Nov. 1864 by U.S. Maj. Gen. John Schofield
8. Gettysburg, PA, 1-3 Jly. 1863 by U.S. Maj. Gen. George Meade, ably assisted by Maj. Gen. John Reynolds and Maj. Gen. Winfield Scott Hancock
9. Drewry's Bluff, VA, 16 May 1864 by C.S. Gen. Pierre G.T. Beauregard
10. Monocacy, MD, 9 Jly. 1864 by U.S. Maj. Gen. Lew Wallace

The Ten Worst Commanded Battles of the War

1. Fort Donelson, TN, 13-16 Feb. 1862 by C.S. Maj. Gen. Gideon Pillow and Brig. Gen. John B. Floyd, with a small assist from Brig. Gen. Simon Bolivar Buckner
2. Fredericksburg, VA, 13 Dec. 1862 by U.S. Maj. Gen. Ambrose Burnside

3. Chancellorsville, VA, 1-4 May 1863 by U.S. Maj. Gen. Joseph Hooker

4. Second Manassas, VA, 29-30 Aug. 1862 by U.S. Maj. Gen. John Pope

5. Murfreesboro/Stones River, TN, 31 Dec. 1862-2 Jan. 1863 by C.S. Gen. Braxton Bragg

6. Gettysburg, PA, 1-3 Jly. 1863 by C.S. Gen. Robert E. Lee

7. Antietam, MD, 17 Sept. 1862 by U.S. Maj. Gen. George McClellan

8. Cold Harbor, VA, 1-3 June 1864 by U.S. Lt. Gen. Ulysses S. Grant

9. Perryville, KY, 8 Oct. 1862 by both C.S. Gen. Braxton Bragg and U.S. Maj. Gen. Don Carlos Buell

10. Chattanooga, TN, 23-25 Nov. 1863 by C.S. Gen. Braxton Bragg

Top Turning Points of the War

1. Ulysses S. Grant given commission of lieutenant general on 9 Mar. 1864 and appointed head general in command of all Union armies.

2. Robert E. Lee appointed to succeed J.E. Johnston as commander of the Army of Northern Virginia 31 May 1862.

3. Battle of Gettysburg, PA, 1-3 Jly. 1863.

4. Battle of First Bull Run, VA, 21 Jly. 1861.

5. Battle of Antietam, MD, 17 Sept. 1862.

6. Grant takes Vicksburg, MS, 4 Jly. 1863

7. Appointment of John B. Hood to succeed Joseph E. Johnston as commander of Army of Tennessee 17 Jly. 1864.

8. Buell arrives at Pittsburg Landing (Shiloh) to save Grant 6 Apr. 1862.

9. Death of Thomas J. "Stonewall" Jackson 10 May 1863.

10. The U.S.S. *Monitor* faces the C.S.S *Virginia* at Hampton Roads on 9 Mar. 1864.

11. Death of General Albert Sidney Johnston at Shiloh, 6 Apr. 1862.

12. New Orleans, LA surrenders to Capt. David G. Farragut on 25 Apr. 1862.
13. Fall of Atlanta, GA to Federal forces on 2 Sept. 1864.
14. Fall of Nashville, TN to Federal forces, Feb. 1862

Ten Most Obvious Victories

Battle	Winner
1. Ezra Church, GA, 28 Jly. 1864	U.S.A.
2. Port Hudson, LA, 27 May 1863	C.S.A.
3. Fort Wagner, SC, 18 Jly. 1863	C.S.A.
4. Atlanta, GA, 22 Jly. 1864	U.S.A.
5. Franklin, TN, 30 Nov. 1864	U.S.A.
6. Gaines' Mill, VA, 27 June 1862	U.S.A.
7. Port Hudson, LA, 14 June 1863	C.S.A.
8. Kennesaw Mountain, GA, 27 June 1864	C.S.A.
9. Jonesborough, GA, 31 Aug.-1 Sept. 1864	U.S.A.
10. Cold Harbor, VA, 1-3 June 1864	C.S.A.

Ten Most Evenly Matched Battles

Battle	U.S.A.	C.S.A.
1. Prairie Grove, AK, 7 Dec. 1862	10,000	10,000
2. Fair Oaks, VA, 31 May-1 June 1862	41,797	41,816
3. Olustee, FL, 20 Feb. 1864	5,115	5,200
4. Franklin, TN, 30 Nov. 1864	27,939	26,897
5. Corinth, MS. 3-4 Oct. 1862	21,147	22,000
6. Richmond, KY, 29-30 Aug. 1862	6,500	6,850
7. Mechanicsville, VA, 26 June 1862	15,631	16,356
8. Bentonville, NC, 19-21 Mar. 1865	16,127	16,895
9. Seven Days, VA, 25 June-1 July, 1862	91,169	95,481
10. Peachtree Creek, GA, 20 July 1864	20,137	18,832

Ten Most Unevenly Matched Battles

Battle	U.S.A.	/ C.S.A. - Ratio
1. Arkansas Post, AK, 10-11 Jan. 1863	28,944	4,564 - 6.34/1
2. Port Hudson, LA, 27 May 1863	13,000	4,192 - 3.10/1
3. Fort Wagner, S.C. 18 July 1863	5,264	1,785 - 2.95/1
4. Hatcher's Run, VA, 5-7 Feb. 1865	34,517	13,835 - .49/1
5. Opequon, VA, 19 Sept. 1864	41,295	17,103 - 2.49/1
6. Perryville, KY, 8 Oct. 1862	36,940	16,000 - 2.31/1
7. Dinwiddie Court House, VA, 31 Mar. '65	45,247	20,030 - 2.26/1
8. Chickasaw Bayou, MS, 27-29 Dec. 1862	30,720	13,792 - 2.23/1
9. Wilson's Creek, MO, 10 Aug. 1861	5,400	11,600 - 1/2.15
10. Nashville, TN, 15-16 Dec. 1864	49,773	23,207 - 2.14/1

Ten Most Unbalanced Battles

Battle	Plurality	Result
1. Appomattox, VA, 9 Apr. 1865	U.S. +62,000	Won
2. Petersburg, VA, 25 Mar. 1865	U.S. +45,000	Won
3. Atlanta, GA, 22 Jly. 1864	U.S. +45,000	Won
4. Fredericksburg, VA, 13 Dec. 1862	U.S. +28,000	Lost
5. Wilderness, VA, 5-7 May 1864	U.S. +27,000	Lost
6. Second Bull Run, VA, 29-30 Aug. 1862	U.S. +27,000	Lost
7. Nashville, TN, 15-16 Dec. 1864	U.S. +26,000	Won
8. Gaines' Mill, VA, 27 June 1862	C.S. +23,000	Lost
9. Vicksburg, MS, 22 May 1863	U.S. +23,000	Lost
10. Shiloh, TN, 6-7 April 1862	U.S. +22,000	Won

CHAPTER 3

GETTYS-BURG

First to Die

First Soldiers Killed at Gettysburg

Confederate: Henry Raison, 7th Tennessee Infantry
Union: Corporal Cyrus W. James, *Co. G., 9th New York Cavalry*

Confederate Strength at Gettysburg

Confederate Engaged Strengths at Gettysburg by State

State	Engaged Troops
Alabama	5,928

Arkansas	479
Florida	739
Georgia	14,147
Louisiana	3,031
Maryland	982
Mississippi	4,930
North Carolina	13,082
South Carolina	4,929
Tennessee	730
Texas	1,250
Virginia	19,034

Confederate Strengths by Corps at Gettysburg

Corps	Troops
Longstreet's First Corps	20,706
Ewell's Second Corps	20,666
Hill's Third Corps	22,083
Stuart's Cavalry	6,621
Total	**70,136**

Confederate Division Strengths at Gettysburg

Division	Troops
Hood's	7,375
McLaws'	6,924
Pickett's	5,473
Johnson's	6,433
Early's	5,460
Rodes'	7,983
Heth's	7,461
Pender's	6,735
R. Anderson's	7,136
Stuart's	6,621

Confederate Losses by State

Confederate Casualties by State at Gettysburg

State	Casualties
Alabama	2,249
Arkansas	182
Florida	455
Georgia	2,703
Louisiana	724
Maryland	228
Mississippi	1,475
North Carolina	6,158
South Carolina	1,308
Tennessee	421
Texas	420
Virginia	4,471

Confederate Percentage Loss by State at Gettysburg

State	% Casualties
Alabama	31.9%
Arkansas	37.9%
Florida	61.6%
Georgia	28.3%
Louisiana	23.9%
Maryland	23.2%
Mississippi	29.9%
North Carolina	43.5%

South Carolina	26.5%
Tennessee	57.7%
Texas	33.6%
Virginia	25.1%
Army	**31.9%**

Confederate Losses by Unit

Confederate Losses by Corps at Gettysburg

Corps	Casualties
Longstreet's First Corps	7,661
Ewell's Third Corps	6,603
Hill's Third Corps	8,007
Stuart's Cavalry	286
Total	**22,557**

Confederate Losses by Division at Gettysburg

Division	Casualties
Hood's	2,371
McLaws'	2,217
Pickett's	2,904
Pender's	2,392
Johnson's	1,936
Early's	1,476
Rodes'	3,116
Heth's	3,358
R. Anderson's	2,158
Stuart's	286

Confederate Divisions Ranked
by Total Loss at Gettysburg

Division	Casualties
1. Heth's	3,358
2. Rodes'	3,116
3. Pickett's	2,904
4. Pender's	2,392
5. Hood's	2,371
6. McLaws'	2,217
7. R. Anderson's	2,158
8. Johnson's	1,936
9. Early's	1,476
10. Stuart's	286

Confederate Divisions Ranked
by Percentage Loss at Gettysburg

Division	% Casualties
1. Pickett's	53.1%
2. Heth's	45.0%
3. Rodes'	39.0%
4. Pender's	35.5%
5. Hood's	32.1%
6. McLaws'	32.0%
7. R. Anderson's	30.2%
8. Johnson's	20.1%
9. Early's	27.0%
10. Stuart's	4.3%

Ten Confederate Brigades with the Greatest Total Loss at Gettysburg

Brigade	Casualties
1. Pettigrew's	1,450
2. Armistead's	1,223
3. Davis'	1,030
4. Daniel's	950
5. R. Garnett's	903
6. Iverson's	903
7. Lane's	792
8. Wilcox's	778
9. Barksdale's	747
10. G. Anderson's	726

Ten Confederate Brigades with Greatest Percentage Loss at Gettysburg

Brigade	% Casualties
1. Iverson's	65.2%
2. R. Garnett's	65.0%
3. Armistead's	62.7%
4. Lang's	61.3%
5. Archer's	57.1%
6. Pettigrew's	56.1%
7. Scales'	50.1%
8. Wright's	49.3%
9. Barksdale's	46.1%
10. Lane's	45.7%

Ten Confederate Infantry Regiments with the Greatest Total Loss at Gettysburg

Regiments	Casualties
1. 26th North Carolina	687
2. 11th North Carolina	366
3. 11th Mississippi	312
4. 5th North Carolina	289
5. 23rd North Carolina	282
6. 8th Alabama	266
7. 42nd Mississippi	265
8. 20th North Carolina	253
9. 18th Virginia	245
10. 28th North Carolina	237

Ten Confederate Infantry Regiments with Greatest Percentage Loss at Gettysburg

Regiment	% Casualties
1. 8th Virginia	92.2%
2. 23rd North Carolina	89.2%
3. 2nd North Carolina Battalion	82.9%
4. 26th North Carolina	81.5%
5. 18th Virginia	78.5%
6. 13th North Carolina	77.2%
7. 13th Alabama	69.5%
8. 9th Virginia	68.9%
9. 28th North Carolina	68.5%
10. 20th North Carolina	68.0%

Eleven Confederate Regiments with the Greatest Number Killed at Gettysburg

Regiment	Killed
1. 26th North Carolina	172
2. 11th North Carolina	108
3. 11th Mississippi	102
4. 42nd Mississippi	75
5. 48th Georgia	69
6. 23rd North Carolina	65
7. 28th North Carolina	65
8. 5th North Carolina	64
9. 45th North Carolina	63
10. 2nd Mississippi	56
11. 1st Maryland Battalion	56

Ten Confederate Infantry Regiments with the Greatest Number of Wounded at Gettysburg

Regiment	Wounded
1. 26th North Carolina	443
2. 11th North Carolina	200
3. 42nd Mississippi	190
4. 14th South Carolina	182
5. 2nd Mississippi	176
6. 11th Mississippi	168
7. 47th North Carolina	159
8. 11th Georgia	156
9. 17th Mississippi	153
10. 8th Alabama	146

Ten Confederate Infantry Regiments with the Greatest Number Missing/Captured at Gettysburg

Regiment	Missing/Captured
1. 13th Alabama	157
2. 20th North Carolina	118
3. 5th North Carolina	100
4. 15th Georgia	99
5. 1st North Carolina	97
6. 23rd North Carolina	97
7. 1st Tennessee	95
8. 15th Alabama	90
9. 9th Virginia	83
10. 8th Alabama	80

Ten Confederate Cavalry Regiments with the Greatest Total Loss at Gettysburg

Regiment	Casualties
1. 1st North Carolina	44
2. 4th Virginia	33
3. 1st Virginia	23
4. Cobb Legion	21
5. 9th Virginia	18
6. 1st Maryland	17
7. 13th Virginia	17
8. 2nd Virginia	16
9. Davis Legion	15
10. 1st South Carolina	14

Eleven Confederate Cavalry Regiments with the Greatest Percentage Loss at Gettysburg

Regiment	% Casualties
1. 1st North Carolina	10.8%
2. 1st Virginia	7.4%
3. Cobb Legion	6.4%
4. 2nd North Carolina	6.2%
5. 4th Virginia	6.1%
6. Davis Legion	6.1%
7. 13th Virginia	5.7%
8. 1st Maryland	5.5%
9. 10th Virginia	5.1%
10. Phillips Legion	4.2%
11. 2nd Virginia	4.2%

Eleven Confederate Batteries with the Greatest Total Loss at Gettysburg

Battery	Casualties
1. Page's Virginia Battery	39
2. Gilbert's South Carolina Battery	36
3. Moody's Louisiana Battery	33
4. Woolfolk's Virginia Battery	28
5. Carpenter's Virginia Battery	24
6. W. Carter's Virginia Battery	23
7. A. Graham's Virginia Battery	21
8. Fraser's Georgia Battery	19
9. Parker's Virginia Battery	18
10. Wingfield's Georgia Battery	17
11. Brander's Virginia Battery	17

Ten Confederate Batteries with Greatest Percentage Loss at Gettysburg

Battery	% Casualties
1. Gilbert's South Carolina Battery	50.7%
2. Page's Virginia Battery	34.2%
3. Fraser's Georgia Battery	30.2%
4. Woolfolk's Virginia Battery	27.7%
5. Carpenter's Virginia Battery	26.4%
6. Brander's Virginia Battery	26.2%
7. A. Graham's Virginia Battery	24.7%
8. Moody's Louisiana Battery	24.4%
9. Brown's Maryland Battery	22.4%
10. W. Carter's Virginia Battery	22.3%

Union Strength at Gettysburg

Union Engaged Strengths by State at Gettysburg

State	Engaged Troops
Connecticut	1,268
Delaware	485
Illinois	1,019
Indiana	2,036
Maine	3,720
Maryland	1,953
Massachusetts	5,793
Michigan	2,649
Minnesota	378
New Hampshire	843

New Jersey	4,039
New York	23,056
Ohio	4,400
Pennsylvania	23,412
Rhode Island	944
United States Regulars	6,306
Vermont	4,358
West Virginia	789
Wisconsin	2,133
Army	**89,581**

Union Strengths by Corps at Gettysburg

Corps	Troops
Army HQ	50
I Corps	12,222
II Corps	11,347
III Corps	10,675
V Corps	10,907
VI Corps	13,596
XI Corps	9,188
XII Corps	9,788
Cavalry Corps	11,851
Artillery Reserve	2,376
Total	**93,693**

Union Losses by State

Union Casualties by State at Gettysburg

State	Casualties
Connecticut	340
Delaware	161

Illinois	139
Indiana	552
Maine	1,024
Maryland	140
Massachusetts	1,537
Michigan	1,111
Minnesota	224
New Hampshire	368
New Jersey	634
New York	6,694
Ohio	1,271
Pennsylvania	5,886
Rhode Island	97
United States Regulars	1,224
Vermont	415
West Virginia	67
Wisconsin	806
Army	**22,656**

Union Percentage Loss by State at Gettysburg

State	% Casualties
Connecticut	25.3%
Delaware	26.8%
Illinois	13.6%
Indiana	27.1%
Maine	27.5%
Maryland	7.2%
Massachusetts	26.5%
Michigan	41.9%
Minnesota	59.3%
New Hampshire	43.7%
New Jersey	15.7%
New York	29.0%
Ohio	28.9%
Pennsylvania	25.1%

Rhode Island	10.3%
United States Regulars	19.4%
Vermont	9.5%
West Virginia	8.5%
Wisconsin	38.8%
Army	**25.3%**

Union Losses by Unit

Union Losses by Corps at Gettysburg

Corps	Casualties
Army HQ	4
I Corps	6,059
II Corps	4,369
III Corps	4,211
V Corps	2,187
VI Corps	242
XI Corps	9,188
XII Corps	1,082
Cavalry Corps	610
Artillery Reserve	242
Total	**22,807**

Ten Union Divisions with Greatest Total Loss at Gettysburg

Division	Casualties
1. Wadsworth's Division (I Corps)	2,155
2. Doubleday's Division (I Corps)	2,103
3. Humphrey's Division (III Corps)	2,092
4. Birney's Division (III Corps)	2,011
5. Robinson's Division (I Corps)	1,960

6. *Gibbon's Division (II Corps)*	1,647
7. *Schurz's Division (XI Corps)*	1,476
8. *Barlow's (XI Corps)*	1,306
9. *Hays' Division (II Corps)*	1,291
10. *Caldwell's Division (II Corps)*	1,275

Ten Union Divisions with Greatest Percentage Loss at Gettysburg

Division	% Casualties
1. *Robinson's Division (I Corps)*	56.4%
2. *Wadsworth's Division (I Corps)*	55.9%
3. *Barlow's Division (XI Corps)*	52.7%
4. *Schurz's Division (XI Corps)*	47.5%
5. *Gibbon's Division (II Corps)*	45.6%
6. *Doubleday's Division (I Corps)*	44.7%
7. *Humphrey's Division (III Corps)*	42.5%
8. *Birney's Division (III Corps)*	39.5%
9. *Caldwell's Division (II Corps)*	38.4%
10. *Hays' Division (II Corps)*	35.4%

Ten Union Brigades with Greatest Total Loss at Gettysburg

Brigade	Casualties
1. *Meredith's Brigade (I Corps)*	1,153
2. *Paul's Brigade (I Corps)*	1,026
3. *Cutler's Brigade (I Corps)*	1,002
4. *Rowley's Brigade (I Corps)*	898
5. *Stone's Brigade (I Corps)*	853
6. *Schimmelfennig's Brigade (XI Corps)*	807
7. *Carr's Brigade (III Corps)*	790
8. *Ward's Brigade (III Corps)*	781
9. *Brewster's Brigade (III Corps)*	778
10. *Ames' Brigade (XI Corps)*	778

Ten Union Brigades with Greatest Percentage Loss at Gettysburg

Brigade	% Casualties
1. *Paul's Brigade (I Corps)*	66.8%
2. *Rowley's Brigade (I Corps)*	66.0%
3. *Stone's Brigade (I Corps)*	64.8%
4. *Meredith's Brigade (I Corps)*	63.0%
5. *Ames' Brigade (I Corps)*	58.2%
6. *Harrow's Brigade (II Corps)*	56.2%
7. *Cutler's Brigade (I Corps)*	49.7%
8. *Coster's Brigade (XI Corps)*	49.1%
9. *Graham's Brigade (III Corps)*	48.8%
10. *Schimmelfennig's Brigade (XI Corps)*	48.0%

Ten Union Infantry Regiments with Greatest Total Loss at Gettysburg

Regiment	Casualties
1. *24th Michigan*	363
2. *151st Pennsylvania*	337
3. *149th Pennsylvania*	336
4. *157th New York*	307
5. *147th New York*	296
6. *150th Pennsylvania*	264
7. *143rd Pennsylvania*	253
8. *134th New York*	252
9. *111th New York*	249
10. *94th New York*	245

Ten Union Infantry Regiments with the Greatest Percentage Loss at Gettysburg

Regiment	% Casualties
1. *154th New York*	83.7%

2. *25th Ohio*	83.6%
3. *16th Maine*	77.9%
4. *147th New York*	77.9%
5. *2nd Wisconsin*	77.2%
6. *157th New York*	75.1%
7. *149th Pennsylvania*	74.7%
8. *24th Michigan*	73.2%
9. *151 Pennsylvania*	72.2%
10. *141 Pennsylvania*	71.3%

Ten Infantry Regiments with the Greatest Number of Killed at Gettysburg

Regiment	Killed
1. *24th Michigan*	67
2. *147th New York*	60
3. *111th New York*	58
4. *149th Pennsylvania*	51
6. *73rd New York*	51
7. *1st Minnesota*	50
8. *82nd New York*	45
9. *72nd New York*	44
10. *134th New York*	42

Ten Union Regiments with the Greatest Number of Wounded at Gettysburg

Regiment	Wounded
1. *24th Michigan*	210
2. *126th New York*	181
3. *111th New York*	177
4. *26th Pennsylvania*	176
5. *1st Minnesota*	173
6. *149th Pennsylvania*	172
7. *19th Maine*	170

8. *157th New York*	166
9. *2nd Wisconsin*	155
10. *120th New York*	154

Eleven Union Infantry Regiments with Greatest Number of Missing/Captured at Gettysburg

Regiment	Missing/Captured
1. *45th New York*	178
2. *154th New York*	178
3. *94th New York*	175
4. *107th Pennsylvania*	165
5. *16th Maine*	164
6. *157th New York*	114
7. *149th Pennsylvania*	111
8. *13th Massachusetts*	101
9. *76th New York*	99
10. *17th Connecticut*	96
11. *75th Ohio*	96

Ten Union Cavalry Regiments with Greatest Total Loss at Gettysburg

Regiment	Casualties
1. *7th Michigan*	100
2. *1st Michigan*	73
3. *1st Vermont*	65
4. *5th Michigan*	56
5. *8th New York*	40
6. *3rd Indiana*	32
7. *6th Michigan*	28
8. *3rd Pennsylvania*	21
9. *12th Illinois*	20
10. *2nd United States*	17

Ten Union Cavalry Regiments with Greatest Percentage Loss at Gettysburg

Regiment	% Casualties
1. *7th Michigan*	26.1%
2. *1st Michigan*	17.1%
3. *1st Vermont*	10.8%
4. *3rd Indiana*	10.2%
5. *5th Michigan*	8.7%
6. *12th Illinois*	8.6%
7. *8th New York*	6.9%
8. *3rd West Virginia*	6.8%
9. *3rd Pennsylvania*	6.3%
10. *6th Michigan*	5.9%

Ten Union Batteries with the Greatest Total Loss at Gettysburg

Battery	Casualties
1. *Battery A, 4th U.S. Artillery*	38
2. *Battery B, 4th U.S. Artillery*	46
3. *Battery A, 1st Rhode Island Artillery*	32
4. *Battery E, 1st Rhode Island Artillery*	30
5. *Battery B, 1st Rhode Island Artillery*	28
6. *9th Massachusetts Battery*	28
7. *Batteries C/F Pennsylvania Artillery*	28
8. *Battery B, 1st New York Artillery*	26
9. *Battery I, 1st United States Artillery*	25
10. *Battery K, 4th United States Artillery*	25

Ten Union Batteries with the Greatest Percentage Loss at Gettysburg

Battery	% Casualties
1. *Battery I, 5th U.S. Artillery*	31.0%

2. *Battery A, 4th U.S. Artillery*   30.2%
3. *Battery B, 4th U.S. Artillery*   29.3%
4. *Battery E, 1st Rhode Island Artillery*   27.8%
5. *Battery A, 1st Rhode Island Artillery*   27.4%
6. *9th Massachusetts Battery*   26.9%
7. *Batteries C/F Pennsylvania Artillery*   26.7%
8. *15th New York Battery*   22.9%
9. *Battery I, 1st New York Artillery*   22.3%
10. *Battery B, 1st New York Artillery*   22.2%

Commanders Killed or Mortally Wounded at Gettysburg

Confederate Generals Killed and Mortally Wounded at Gettysburg

Maj. Gen. William D. Pender (mortally wounded)
Brig. Gen. Lewis Armistead
Brig. Gen. William Barksdale
Brig. Gen. Richard B. Garnett
Brig. Gen. Paul J. Semmes (mortally wounded)

Union Generals and Brigade Commanders Killed at Gettysburg

Maj. Gen. John F. Reynolds
Brig. Gen. Elon J. Farnsworth
Brig. Gen. Stephen H. Weed
Brig. Gen. Samuel K. Zook

Col. Strong Vincent
Col. Edward F. Cross
Col. George L. Williard
Col. Eliakim Sherrill

Burials at Gettysburg

Burials by Section in the Gettysburg National Cemetery

State	Burials
Connecticut	22
Delaware	15
Illinois	6 plus 4 postwar
Indiana	81
Maine	104
Maryland	21
Massachusetts	159
Michigan	175
Minnesota	56
New Hampshire	49
New Jersey	79
New York	876
Ohio	131 plus 3 postwar
Pennsylvania	575
Rhode Island	14
United States Regulars	140
Vermont	61
West Virginia	11
Wisconsin	73
Unknown	979
Unknown	3,627

Source: *The Last Full Measure, Burials in the Soldier's National Cemetery,* by John W. Busey, used with permission.

CHAPTER 4

CASUALTIES

Bloodiest Battles

Ten Bloodiest Battles (Combined Casualties)

Battle	Total Casualties
1. Gettysburg	40,638
2. Chickamauga	28,399
3. Seven Days	27,535
4. Antietam	23,381
5. Wilderness	22,033
6. Chancellorsville	21,862
7. Shiloh	17,897
8. Atlanta	19,715
9. Second Mannasas	19,204
10. Stones River	18,459

Confederate Losses by State

Confederate Battle Deaths by State

State	Deaths
Alabama	742
Arkansas	3,080
Florida	1,299
Georgia	7,272
Louisiana	3,486
Mississippi	8,458
North Carolina	19,673
South Carolina	12,922
Tennessee	2,989
Texas	2,589
Virginia	7,847
Border States	2,692
Regular Army	1,448
Total	**74,524**

Confederate Deaths from Disease by State

State	Deaths
Alabama	724
Arkansas	3,782
Florida	1,047
Georgia	3,702
Louisiana	3,059
Mississippi	6,807
North Carolina	20,602
South Carolina	4,760
Tennessee	3,425

Texas	1,260
Virginia	6,947
Border States	2,142
Regular Army	1,040
Total	**59,297**

Note: Confederate War Department Records were very incomplete and the actual total was probably far higher, such as suggested by the disparity between figures for North Carolina and the Regular Army.

Confederate Losses in Battle

Ten Bloodiest Battles for the Confederates

Battle	Total Killed & Wounded
1. Gettysburg	22,638
2. Seven Days	19,739
3. Chickamauga	16,986
4. Antietam	11,724
5. Chancellorsville	10,746
6. Shiloh	9,735
7. Stones River	9,239
8. Atlanta	9,187
9. Second Manassas	9,108
10. Wilderness	7,750

Ten Proportionately Bloodiest Battles (Confederate Casualties Per 1,000 Troops)

Battle	Casualties/1,000 Troops
1. Gettysburg	301
2. Stones River	266
3. Chickamauga	259
4. Shiloh	241
5. Antietam	226

6. Jonesborough   222
7. Seven Days   207
8.-9.
   Franklin   206
   Tupelo   206
10. Perryville   196

Ten Proportionately Least Bloodiest Battles (Confederate Casualties Per 1,000)

Battle	Casualties/1,000 Troops
1. Port Hudson (14 June 1863)	13
2. Chickasaw Bayou	14
3.-4.	
Mine Run	15
Kennesaw Mountain	15
5. Arkansas Post	24
6. Hatcher's Run	39
7. Pea Ridge	43
8. Williamsburg	49
9. Chattanooga	55
10. Port Hudson (27 May 1863)	56

Confederate Unit Losses

Ten Confederate Brigades with the Greatest Percentage Loss in a Single Action

Brigade	Battle	% Loss
1. Garnett's	Gettysburg	65.9%
2. Perry's	Gettysburg	65.0%
3. Wofford's	Antietam	64.1%
4. R.H. Anderson's	Seven Days	62.9%

5. Pryor's	Seven Days	61.5%
6. Cockrell's	Franklin	60.2%
7. Wilcox's	Seven Days	57.0%
8. Benning's	Chickamauga	56.6%
9. Ramseur's	Chancellorsville	52.2%
10. Bates'	Chickamauga	51.1%

Ten Confederate Regiments with the Greatest Percentage Loss in a Single Action

Regiment	Battle	% Casualties
1. 1st Texas	Antietam	82.3%
2. 21st Georgia	Second Manassas	76.0%
3. 26th North Carolina	Gettysburg	71.7%
4. 6th Mississippi	Shiloh	70.5%
5. 8th Tennessee	Stones River	68.2%
6. 10th Tennessee	Chickamauga	68.0%
7. Palmetto Sharpshooters (S.C.)	Glendale	67.7%
8. 17th South Carolina	Second Manassas	66.9%
9. 23rd South Carolina	Second Manassas	66.2%
10. 44th Georgia	Mechanicsville	65.1%

Union Losses by State

Total Union Deaths by State

State	Deaths
Alabama	345
Arkansas	1,713
California	573
Colorado Territory	323
Connecticut	5,354
Dakota Territory	6

Delaware	882
District of Columbia	290
Florida	215
Georgia	15
Illinois	34,834
Indiana	26,672
Iowa	13,001
Kansas	2,630
Kentucky	10,774
Louisiana	945
Maine	9,398
Maryland	2,982
Massachusetts	13,942
Michigan	14,753
Minnesota	2,584
Mississippi	78
Missouri	13,885
Nebraska Territory	239
Nevada	33
New Hampshire	4,882
New Jersey	5,754
New Mexico Territory	277
New York	46,534
North Carolina	360
Ohio	35,475
Oregon	45
Pennsylvania	33,183
Rhode Island	1,321
Tennessee	6,777
Texas	141
Vermont	5,224
Virginia	42
Washington Territory	22
West Virginia	4,017
Wisconsin	12,301

Union Army Losses

Union Deaths From All Causes

Cause	Deaths
Died in Battle or from Wounds	110,070
Died of Disease	199,720
Prisons	24,866
Cause Not Known	12,121
Drowning	4,944
Accidents	4,114
Miscellaneous	2,034
Murdered	520
Suicide	391
Sunstroke	313
Military Executions	267
Killed after Capture	104
Executed by the Enemy	64

Summary of Union Army Killed and Mortally Wounded

Command	Deaths
Volunteers	104,893
Regulars	2,283
Colored Troops	2,894
Total	**110,070**

Total Number of Union Killed and Wounded by Branch of Service

Branch of Service	Deaths
Infantry	96,885
Sharpshooters	466
Cavalry	10,596
Light Artillery	1,817
Heavy Artillery	129
Engineers	76
Generals	67
Staff	18
Miscellaneous	16
Total	110,070

Summary of Union Deaths by Disease

Command	Deaths
Volunteers	167,510
Regulars	2,552
Colored Troops	29,658
Total	199,720

Union Losses in Battle

Ten Bloodiest Battles for the Union

Battle	Total Killed & Wounded
1. Gettysburg	17,684
2. Wilderness	14,283
3. Spotsylvania	12,632
4. Cold Harbor	12,000
5. Antietam	11,657

6. Chickamauga	11,413
7. Chancellorsville	11,116
8. Fredericksburg	10,884
9. Atlanta	10,528
10. Shiloh	10,162

Ten Proportionately Bloodiest Battles
(Union Casualties Per 1,000 Troops)

Battle	Casualties/1,000 Troops
1. Port Hudson (14 June 1863)	267
2. Olustee	265
3. Stones River	223
4. Cedar Mountain	219
5. Fort Wagner	214
6. Gettysburg	212
7. Chickamauga	196
8.-9.	
Wilson's Creek	175
Drewry's Bluff (12 May 1864)	175
10. Shiloh	162

Ten Proportionately Least Bloodiest Battles
(Union Casualties Per 1,000 Troops)

Battle	Casualties/1,000 Troops
1. Jonesborough	13
2.-3.	
Mechanicsville	16
Mine Run	16
4. Boydton Plank Road	28
5. Chickasaw Bayou	39
6. Franklin	40
7. Ezra Church	42

8.-9.

Tupelo	45
Williamsburg	45
10. Dinwiddie Court House	48

Ten Battles with the Lowest Proportion of Union Wounded to Killed

Battle	Proportion of Wounded to Killed
1. Williamsburg	3.0
2. Perryville	3.3
3. Fort Wagner	3.5
4. Crampton's Gap	3.6
5. Kernstown	3.8
6. Rappahannock Station	3.9
7. Fort Donelson	4.2
8. New Berne	4.2
9. Fair Oaks	4.5
10. North Anna	4.6

Ten Battles with Highest Proportion of Union Wounded to Killed

Battle	Proportion of Wounded to Killed
1. Arkansas Post	6.7
2. Mine Run	6.3
3. Missionary Ridge	6.2
4. Opequon Creek	5.7
5. Deep Bottom	5.6
6. Mill Springs	5.3
7. Wilderness	5.3
8. Corinth	5.1
9. Atlanta	5.1
10. Spotsylvania	4.9

Nine Eastern Campaigns with Greatest Union Loss in Cavalry

Campaigns	Casualties
1. Shenandoah Valley, 1864	3,917
2. Gettysburg	3,408
3. Trevilian Raid	1,512
4. Appomattox	1,490
5. Wilson's Cavalry Raid, 1864	1,452
6. Beverly Ford	866
7. Wilderness	849
8. Hawe's Shop	656
9. Yellow Tavern	625

Union Unit Losses

Ten Union Infantry Regiments with the Greatest Percentage Loss in a Single Action

Regiment	Battle	% Casualties
1. *1st Minnesota*	Gettysburg	82.0%
2. *141 Pennsylvania*	Gettysburg	75.7%
3. *101st New York*	Second Manassas	73.8%
4. *25th Massachusetts*	Cold Harbor	70.0%
5. *36th Wisconsin*	Bethesda Church	69.0%
6. *20th Massachusetts*	Fredericksburg	68.4%
7. *8th Vermont*	Cedar Creek	67.9%
8. *81st Pennsylvania*	Fredericksburg	67.4%
9. *12th Massachusetts*	Antietam	67.0%
10. *1st Maine Heavy Artillery*	Petersburg	66.5%

Ten Union Infantry Regiments with the Most Battle Deaths

Regiment	Battle Deaths
1. 5th New Hampshire	295
2. 83rd Pennsylvania	282
3. 7th Wisconsin	281
4. 5th Michigan	263
5. 20th Massachusetts	260
6. 69th New York	259
7. 28th Massachusetts	250
8. 16th Michigan	247
9. 105th Pennsylvania	245
10. 6th Wisconsin	244

Ten Union Infantry Regiments with the Maximum Number of Battle Deaths (Percentage of Enrollment)

Regiment	Battle Deaths
1. 2nd Wisconsin	19.7%
2. 1st Maine Heavy Artillery	19.2%
3. 57th Massachusetts	19.1%
4. 140th Pennsylvania	17.4%
5. 26th Wisconsin	17.2%
6. 7th Wisconsin	17.2%
7. 69th New York	17.1%
8. 11th Pennsylvania Reserves	16.6%
9. 142nd Pennsylvania	16.5%
10. 141st Pennsylvania	16.1%

Ten Union Infantry Regiments with Most Battle Deaths in a Single Action

Regiment	Battle	Battle Deaths
1. *5th New York*	Second Manassas	117
2. *15th New Jersey*	Spotsylvania	116
3. *49th Pennsylvania*	Spotsylvania	109
4. *15th Massachusetts*	Antietam	108
5. *1st Kansas*	Wilson's Creek	106
6.-7.		
1st Missouri	Wilson's Creek	103
9th Illinois	Shiloh	103
8.-9.		
18th United States	Stones River	102
11th Illinois	Fort Donelson	102
10. *121st New York*	Salem Church	97

Twelve Union Infantry Regiments with the Greatest Percentage of Battle Deaths in a Single Action

Regiment	Battle	Deaths
1. *1st Minnesota*	Gettysburg	28%
2. *15th New Jersey*	Spotsylvania	26%
3. *141 Pennsylvania*	Gettysburg	24%
4. *10th United States*	Gettysburg	23%
5. *79th United States Colored Troops*	Poison Springs	23%
6. *25th Massachusetts*	Cold Harbor	23%
7. *5th New York*	Second Manassas	23%
8. *49th Pennsylvania*	Spotsylvania	22%
9. *1st Maine Artillery*	Petersburg	22%
10. *12th Massachusetts*	Antietam	22%
11. *69th New York*	Antietam	22%
12. *11th New York*	Gettysburg	22%

Ten Union Regiments with the Maximum Number of Officers Killed in the War

Regiment	Officers Killed
1. *1st Maine Heavy Artillery*	23
2. *61st Pennsylvania*	19
3. *8th New York Heavy Artillery*	19
4. *5th New Hampshire*	18
5. *12th Massachusetts*	18
6. *48th New York*	18
7. *73rd New York*	18
8. *81st Pennsylvania*	18
9. *145th Pennsylvania*	18
10. *31st Maine*	18

Nine Union Heavy Artillery Regiments with the Most Battle Deaths

Regiment	Deaths
1. *1st Maine*	423
2. *8th New York*	361
3. *7th New York*	291
4. *2nd Connecticut*	254
5. *1st Massachusetts*	241
6. *2nd Pennsylvania*	233
7. *14th New York*	226
8. *2nd New York*	214
9. *9th New York*	204

Ten Union Heavy Artillery Regiments with the Most Deaths in a Single Action

Regiment	Battle	Deaths
1. *1st Maine*	Petersburg	210
2. *8th New York*	Cold Harbor	207

3. *1st Maine*	Spotsylvania	147
4. *2nd Connecticut*	Cold Harbor	129
5. *7th New York*	Cold Harbor	127
6. *1st Massachusetts*	Spotsylvania	120
7. *9th New York*	Cedar Creek	64
8. *2nd Pennsylvania*	Petersburg	64
9. *14th New York*	Petersburg	57
10. *7th New York*	Petersburg	55

Ten Union Volunteer Artillery Batteries with Most Battle Deaths in the War

Regiments	Deaths
1. *Battery B, 1st Pennsylvania Artillery*	21
2. *11th Ohio Battery*	20
3. *5th Massachusetts Battery*	19
4. *Battery C., 1st Rhode Island Artillery*	19
5. *1st New York Battery*	18
6. *5th Maine Battery*	18
7. *Battery F, 1st Pennsylvania Artillery*	18
8. *Battery A, 1st Pennsylvania Artillery*	17
9. *Battery G, 1st Pennsylvania Artillery*	17
10. *Battery E, 1st Rhode Island Artillery*	17

Twelve Union Light Artillery Batteries with the Greatest Loss in a Single Action

Battery	Battle	Casualties
1. *11th Ohio Battery*	Iuka	54
2. *Battery K, 4th U.S. Artillery*	Chancellorsville	45
3. *Battery H, 5th U.S. Artillery*	Chickamauga	44
4. *Battery B, 4th U.S. Artillery*	Antietam	40
5. *Battery I, 4th U.S. Artillery*	Chaplin Hills	39
6. *Battery E, 3rd U.S. Artillery*	Olustee	39
7. *Battery A, 4th U.S. Artillery*	Gettysburg	38

8. *Battery B, 4th U.S. Artillery*	Gettysburg	36
9. *Battery M, 1st U.S. Artillery*	Olustee	32
10. *Battery A., 1st Illinois Artillery*	Shiloh	30
11. *14th Ohio Battery*	Shiloh	30
12. *Battery E., 1st Rhode Island Artillery*	Gettysburg	30

Nine Union Cavalry Regiments with Most Battle Deaths

Regiment	Deaths
1. *1st Maine*	174
2. *1st Michigan*	164
3. *5th Michigan*	141
4. *6th Michigan*	135
5. *1st Vermont*	134
6. *1st New York Dragoons*	130
7. *1st New Jersey*	128
8. *2nd New York*	121
9. *11th Pennsylvania*	119

Ten Union Regiments with the Greatest Loss by Death in Confederate Prisons

Regiment	Deaths
1. *2nd Tennessee Infantry*	382
2. *85th New York Infantry*	222
3. *7th New York Heavy Artillery*	204
4. *7th Tennessee Cavalry*	193
5. *103rd Pennsylvania Infantry*	181
6. *2nd Massachusetts Heavy Artillery*	173
7. *1st Vermont Heavy Artillery*	167
8. *101st Pennsylvania Infantry*	158
9. *16th Illinois Cavalry*	157
10. *1st Vermont Cavalry*	149

CHAPTER 5

GENERALS

Generals With Service Before the Civil War

Eight Generals Who Had Served in the War of 1812

1. U.S. Maj. Gen. John A. Dix, fought at Lundy's Lane as a 14 year old ensign.
2. U.S. Brig. Gen. James W. Ripley, U.S.M.A. '14, served as a lieutenant of artillery on the Great Lakes in the last months of the war.
3. U.S. Maj. Gen. and Brevet Lt. Gen. Winfield Scott was a regular army lieutenant colonel at the start of the war, commanded a brigade at both Chippewea and Lundy's Lane, and emerged as a regular army brigadier general and brevet major general.
4. U.S. Brig. Gen. Joseph P. Taylor, brother of Zachary Taylor, enlisted at the start of the war and emerged from it as an infantry lieutenant.
5. U.S. Brig. Gen. Charles M. Thurston, graduating from West Point in 1813, served as an infantry officer.
6. U.S. Brig. Gen. Joseph G. Totten had been a captain of

engineers, winning brevets as major and lieutenant colonel.
7. C.S. Brig. Gen. David E. Twiggs was a regular army captain at the start of the war and emerged from it as a major.
8. U.S. Maj. Gen. John E. Wool volunteered for service on the outbreak of the war and emerged from it as Lt. Col. of the 6th Infantry.

A Baker's Dozen of Confederate Generals Who Were Seminole Veterans

Over 150 men who later served as generals during the Civil War—Union and Confederate—were veterans of the long series of wars with the Seminoles in Florida (1817-1858), a war that ultimately the Seminoles won.

1. Gen. Braxton Bragg
2. Gen. Samuel Cooper
3. Lt. Gen. Jubal Early
4. Lt. Gen. William Hardee
5. Lt. Gen. Ambrose P. Hill
6. Lt. Gen. Thomas J. Jackson
7. Maj. Gen. Bushrod Johnson
8. Gen. Joseph E. Johnston
9. Lt. Gen. James Longstreet
10. Maj. Gen. John B. Magruder
11. Maj. Gen. John Pegram
12. Lt. Gen. John S. Pemberton
13. Maj. Gen. Earl Van Dorn

A Score of Notable Union Generals Who Fought in the Seminole Wars

1. Maj. Gen. Robert Anderson
2. Maj. Gen. Don Carlos Buell
3. Maj. Gen. Abner Doubleday
4. Maj. Gen. Darius Couch
5. Maj. Gen Edward R. S. Canby
6. Maj. Gen. John Gibbon
7. Maj. Gen. Robert S. Granger
8. Maj. Gen. Winfield Scott Hancock
9. Maj. Gen. Ethan Allan Hitchcock
10. Maj. Gen. Oliver O. Howard
11. Maj. Gen. Andrew A. Humphreys
12. Brig. Gen. Nathaniel Lyon
13. Maj. Gen. Edward O.C. Ord
14. Maj. Gen. Alfred Pleasonton
15. Maj. Gen. John Reynolds
16. Maj. Gen. (and Brevet Lt. Gen.) Winfield Scott
17. Maj. Gen. John Sedgwick
18. Maj. Gen. Henry W Slocum
19. Maj. Gen. George Sykes
20. Maj. Gen. George H. Thomas

Ten Veterans of the Black Hawk War Who Became Prominent during the Civil War

1. U.S. Maj. Gen. Robert Anderson
2. U.S. Brig. Gen. Edward D. Baker
3. U.S. Brig. Gen. James Barnes
4. U.S. Brig. Gen. Philip St. George Cooke
5. C.S. Maj. Gen. George B. Crittenden
6. C.S. Gen. Albert Sidney Johnston
7. C.S. Gen. Joseph E. Johnston
8. U.S. President Abraham Lincoln

9. U.S. Maj. Gen. John A. McClernand

10. Maj. Gen. Edwin Vose Sumner

In April of 1832 about 500 Sauk and Fox warriors, accompanied by numerous women and children, crossed the Mississippi into northern Illinois, seeking to regain ancestral homelands which had been promised them under a treaty dating from 1804. Within weeks some 6,800 troops, regulars, volunteers, and militia, were mobilized to put suppress the "invasion," which was accomplished by early August. Several of the men who took part in this campaign later rose to some prominence during the Civil War, including about 30 who became generals.

Ten Confederate Generals
Who Soldiered for Texas, 1835-1845

1. Brig. Gen. William W. Adams served as a volunteer in 1839.

2. Brig. Gen. Henry W. Allen served during the Texas Revolution.

3. Maj. Gen. George B. Crittenden was a Texas regular army officer, 1837-1842.

4. Brig. Gen. James M. Goggin was a lieutenant in the Texas Army in 1842.

5. Brig. Gen. Thomas Green was an artilleryman who fought at San Jacinto.

6. Brig. Gen. Joseph L. Hogg was a Texas militiaman, 1839-1842.

7. Gen. Albert Sidney Johnston enlisted as a private in the Texas Army in 1837, was almost immediately promoted Brigadier General, and in 1838 became Secretary of War, resigning two years later.

8. Brig. Gen. Walker P. Lane was an infantryman at San Jacinto.

9. Brig. Gen. Ben McCulloch was an artilleryman who fought alongside Green at San Jacinto.

10. Brig. Gen. Jerome Bonaparte Robertson, Texas volunteer, 1836.

One Union General
Who Soldiered for the Republic of Texas

1. Brig. Gen. George Washington Morgan served as an infantry officer during the Texas Revolution.

Nine Notable Civil War Generals
Who *Did Not* See Action in the Mexican War

1. C.S. Maj. Gen. Henry Heth
2. U.S. Maj. Gen. Andrew A. Humphreys
3. U.S. Maj. Gen. John Newton
4. C.S. Brig. Gen. William Pendleton
5. U.S. Maj. Gen. Joseph J. Reynolds
6. U.S. Maj. Gen. William Rosecrans
7. U.S. Maj. Gen. William Tecumseh Sherman
8. U.S. Maj. Gen. William F. Smith
9. C.S. Maj. Gen. Isaac Trimble

Over 200 of the 1,008 men who became generals during the Civil War saw no field service during the War with Mexico. Some of these men were living abroad at the time and some were too young to serve or were not in the army at all. The men listed here were in the army, but were posted far from active theaters of operations.

Ten "Red '48-ers" Who Became Union
Generals in the Civil War

1. Brig. Gen. Alexander S. Asboth, a veteran of the Hungarian Revolution.
2. Brig. Gen. Louis Blenker, a veteran of the Revolution in Hesse-Darmstadt.
3. Brig. Gen. Charles Matthias, a veteran of the Prussian Revolution.
4. Brig. Gen. Peter J. Osterhaus, the Prussian Revolution.
5. Maj. Gen. Carl Schurz, was a veteran of the Baden Revolution.

6. Brig. Gen. Alexander Schimmelfennig, a Prussian regular officer, had also joined the revolutionaries in Baden.
7. Brig. Gen. Albin F. Schoepf, veteran of the Hungarian Revolution.
8. Maj. Gen. Franz Sigel, veteran of the German Revolution.
9. Brig. Gen. Max Weber, the Baden Revolution.
10. Brig. Gen. August von Villich, also from Baden.

One Union General Who Fought *Against* the "Red '48-ers"

1. Brig. Gen. Gustave P. Cluseret, earned the Legion of Honor for helping to suppress the "July Revolution" in France.

Five Crimean War Veterans Who Became Generals in the Civil War

1. William M. Browne, an Irishman, claimed to have served as an officer in the British Army in the Crimea, a matter which cannot be proven and about which there is some doubt, but did become a brigadier general in the Confederate Army.
2. Gustave P. Cluseret served as a captain in the French cavalry before joining Garibaldi's forces in 1860, and joined the Union Army in early 1862, rising to brigadier general.
3. Camille Armand Jules Marie, the Prince de Polignac, was an officer with the French 4th Hussars in the Crimea, later migrating to the U.S., where he joined the Confederate Army and rose to major general.
4. Ivan Vasilovitch Turchinoff, a colonel of the Russian Imperial Guard and fortification engineer, migrated to the U.S. in 1856, volunteered for the Union in 1861 and as "John B. Turchin" rose to brigadier general of volunteers.
5. Edward A. Wild, a physician, served as a surgeon with the Turkish Army during the war, soon afterwards returning to the United States, where he enlisted in the Union Army

in 1861 and rose to brigadier general of volunteers on his merits as a combat officer.

Thirteen Alumni of the Old *2nd Cavalry* Who Became Generals in the Civil War

1. Col. Albert Sidney Johnston, later a full general in the Confederate Army.
2. Lt. Col. Robert E. Lee, later a full general of the Confederacy.
3. Maj. George H. Thomas, later a Union major general.
4. Maj. Earl Van Dorn, later a Confederate major general.
5. Maj. William Hardee, later a Confederate lieutenant general.
6. Capt. Edmund Kirby Smith, later a full general in the Confederate Army.
7. Capt. George Stoneman, later a Union major general.
8. Capt. Richard W. Johnson, later a Union major general.
9. Capt. Innis W. Palmer, later a Union brigadier general.
10. Lt. Frank C. Armstrong, later a Confederate brigadier general.
11. Lt. John B. Hood, later a Confederate full general.
12. Lt. Fitzhugh Lee, later a Confederate lieutenant general.
13. Lt. James P. Majors, later a Confederate brigadier general.

Twenty Prominent Civil War Generals Who Served in the So-Called "Mormon War"

During the 1850s serious tensions arose between the United States and the Mormon community in Utah, which was suspected of harboring a desire to separate itself from the United States. Ultimately, Army was sent into Utah to restore order and the authority of the United States. Nearly 50 veterans of the Utah expedition later became generals during the Civil War, counting both Federals and Confederates, the latter of whom apparently did not see the humor inherent in their having previously served to suppress the Mormon attempt at secession.

Ten Confederate Generals
Who Served in the "Mormon War"

1. Brig. Gen. Barnard E. Bee
2. Brig. Gen. James Deshler
3. Maj. Gen. John H. Forney
4. Brig. Gen. Richard B. Garnett
5. Lt. Gen. William Hardee
6. Gen. Albert Sidney Johnston
7. Gen. Robert E. Lee
8. Maj. Gen. Lafayette McLaws
9. Brig. Gen. John Pegram
10. Lt. Gen. John Pemberton

Ten Union Generals
Who Were Veterans of the "Mormon War"

1. Maj. Gen. Don Carlos Buell
2. Brig. Gen. John Buford
3. Brig. Gen. Philip St. George Cooke
4. Brig. Gen. Elon John Farnsworth
5. Maj. Gen. Winfield Scott Hancock
6. Maj. Gen. John Newton
7. Maj. Gen. Fitz John Porter
8. Maj. Gen. Jesse L. Reno
9. Maj. Gen. John Reynolds
10. Maj. Gen. George H. Thomas

Fourteen Civil War Generals
Who Had Served in "Bleeding Kansas"

1. C.S. Lt. Gen. Richard Anderson
2. U.S. Brig. Gen. Philip St. George Cooke
3. C.S. Brig. Gen. Richard B. Garnett
4. U.S. Brig. Gen. George Washington Getty
5. U.S. Brig. Gen. Albion P. Howe
6. C.S. Lt. Gen. S. D. Lee

7. C.S. Brig. Gen. Armistead Long
8. C.S. Lt. Gen. James Longstreet
9. U.S. Brig. Gen. Nathaniel Lyon
10. U.S. Maj. Gen. Alfred Pleasonton
11. C.S. Maj. Gen. Robert Ransom
12. C.S. Brig. Gen. Joseph O. Shelby
13. U.S. Maj. Gen. T.J. Wood
14. C.S. Brig. Gen. Henry H. Walker

All of these men served as army officers helping to suppress the disorders in Kansas in the late 1850s, except Joseph O. Shelby, a civilian who led a band of pro-slavery ruffians during the troubles.

Five Generals Who Were Veterans of the Capture of John Brown at Harper's Ferry in 1859

1. Lt. Col. Robert E. Lee, later Gen., C.S.A., commanded the Marines who captured John Brown.
2. Lt. James B. Fry, later Brig. Gen., C.S.A.
3. Lt. Albion P. Howe, later Brig. Gen., U.S.A.
4. Lt. James E. B. Stuart, later Lt. Gen., C.S.A., served as a volunteer aide-de-camp to Lee.
5. Lt. William Terry of the Virginia militia, later Brig. Gen., C.S.A.

West Point Generals

The Generals Listed by West Point Class and Rank

West Point was the *alma mater* of most of the senior military commanders on both sides in war. Academy graduates and drop-outs accounted for 156 of the Confederacy's 425 generals (36.7%)

and 228 of the Union's 583 generals (39.1%): in addition, one graduate of Annapolis became a Union general (.0017%).

For each year, the total number of graduates is shown in parentheses. Each man is listed according to his standing in the graduating class, except that before 1818 the listing merely shows the order in which the men graduated, class standings not yet having been introduced.

Men who dropped out are denoted by an asterisk (*) followed by a letter indicating their status at the time they left the Academy: a = "freshman" ("fourth class"), b = "sophomore" ("third class"), and so forth.

To really understand who went to school with whom, it is important to realize that after 1818, when a four year curriculum was introduced, a cadet's tour at West Point spanned seven classes, his own plus the three which graduated immediately prior to it and immediately after it. However in 1854 the Academy course was lengthened to five years by a decision of Secretary of War Jefferson Davis (Class of '28). Cadets entering in that year were divided into two groups: those over 18 were given a four year course, graduating in 1858, while those under 18 were subject to the new five year program, and graduated in 1859. The curriculum was changed back to four years on the eve of the Civil War, and, as a result, there were two graduations in 1861: the May class having entered the Academy in 1856, and the June class in 1857. As a result, the men subject to the five year program—the 1859, 1860, and May 1861 graduates—would have known cadets in a total of eight classes, as would be the case for a small a number of cadets who took more than the normal four years to graduate, such as Joseph K.F. Mansfield, Philip Sheridan, James W. Forsyth, Israel B. Richardson, and John B.S. Todd.

1805 (3)

3rd U.S. Brig. Gen. Joseph G. Totten

1808 (15)

[3rd U.S. Col. Sylvanus Thayer, "The Father of the Military Academy."]

1814 (30)

12th U.S. Brig. Gen. James Wolfe Ripley

15th U.S. Brig. Gen. Charles M. Thurston

1815 (40)

36th C.S. Gen. Samuel Cooper

1817 (19)

17th U.S. Maj. Gen. Ethan Allen Hitchcock

1818 (23)

1st U.S. Brig. Gen. Richard Delafield

1819 (29)

14th U.S. Brig. Gen. Daniel Tyler

1820 (30)

11th C.S. Brig. Gen. John H. Winder
26th U.S. Brig. Gen. George D. Ramsey

1822 (40)

2nd U.S. Maj. Gen. Joseph K. F. Mansfield
17th C.S. Maj. Gen. Isaac R. Trimble
24th U.S. Brig. Gen. George Wright
25th U.S. Maj. Gen. David Hunter
26th U.S. Brig. Gen. George A. McCall
37th U.S. Brig. Gen. John J. Abercrombie

1823 (35)

2nd U.S. Brig. Gen. George S. Greene
17th U.S. Brig. Gen. Lorenzo Thomas

1824 (31)

[1st U.S. Col. Dennis Hart Mahan, distinguished West Point
    instructor and father of Alfred Thayer Mahan.]
[3rd U.S. Capt. Robert P. Parrott, artillery expert.]

1825 (37)

5th C.S. Maj. Gen. Daniel S. Donelson
8th C.S. Maj. Gen. Benjamin Huger
15th U.S. Maj. Gen. Robert Anderson
19th U.S. Maj. Gen. Charles F. Smith
28th U.S. Brig. Gen. William R. Montgomery

1826 (41)

8th C.S. Gen. Albert Sidney Johnston
17th U.S. Maj. Gen. Samuel P. Heintzelman
22nd C.S. Brig. Gen. John B. Grayson
36th U.S. Brig. Gen. Amos B. Eaton
39th U.S. Maj. Gen. Silas Casey

1827 (38)

6th U.S. Brig. Gen. Napoleon B. Buford
8th C.S. Lt. Gen. Leonidas Polk
13th C.S. Brig. Gen. Gabriel James Rains
23rd U.S. Brig. Gen. Philip St. George Cooke

1828 (33)

3rd C.S. Brig. Gen. Hugh W. Mercer
[23rd Jefferson Davis, President of the Confederacy]
28th C.S. Brig. Gen. Thomas F. Drayton

1829 (46)

2nd C.S. Gen. Robert E. Lee
5th U.S. Brig. Gen. James Barnes
6th U.S. Brig. Gen. Catharinus P. Buckingham
13th C.S. Gen. Joseph E. Johnston
15th U.S. Maj. Gen. Ormsby McK. Mitchel
25th U.S. Brig. Gen. Thomas A. Davies
26th C.S. Brig. Gen. Albert G. Blanchard
*b C.S. Brig. Gen. Benjamin G. Humphreys

1830 (42)

5th C.S. Brig. Gen. William N. Pendleton
15th C.S. Maj. Gen. John B. Magruder
31st U.S. Brig. Gen. Robert C. Buchanan
[*b Edgar Allan Poe]

1831 (33)

12th U.S. Brig. Gen. Jacob Ammen
13th U.S. Brig. Gen. Andrew A. Humphreys
14th U.S. Maj. Gen. William H. Emory
19th U.S. Brig. Gen. Thomas J. McKean
22nd C.S. Brig. Gen. Lucius N. Northrop
24th U.S. Brig. Gen. Horatio P. Van Cleve
27th U.S. Maj. Gen. Samuel R. Curtis

1832 (45)

6th C.S. Brig. Gen. Philip St. George Cocke
10th U.S. Maj. Gen. Erasmus Darwin Keyes
26th C.S. Maj. Gen. George B. Crittenden
29th U.S. Brig. Gen. Randolph B. Marcy
35th C.S. Brig. Gen. Richard G. Gatlin
42nd C.S. Brig. Gen. Humphrey Marshall

1833 (43)

2nd U.S. Brig. Gen. John G. Barnard
3rd U.S. Brig. Gen. George W. Cullum
4th U.S. Brig. Gen. Rufus King
14th C.S. Brig. Gen. Henry C. Wayne
22nd U.S. Brig. Gen. Benjamin Alvord
29th U.S. Brig. Gen. Henry W. Wessells
34th C.S. Brig. Gen. Daniel Ruggles

1834 (36)

4th U.S. Brig. Gen. Thomas A. Morris
18th U.S. Brig. Gen. Gabriel R. Paul

25th C.S. Brig. Gen. Goode Bryan
32nd U.S. Brig. Gen. William S. Ketchum

1835 (56)

1st U.S. Maj. Gen. George W. Morell
3rd U.S. Brig. Gen. John H. Martindale
17th U.S. Brig. Gen. James H. Stokes
[18th Montgomery Blair, Lincoln's Postmaster General]
19th U.S. Maj. Gen. George G. Meade
23rd U.S. Brig. Gen. Henry M. Naglee
30th U.S. Brig. Gen. Henry Prince
31st U.S. Brig. Gen. Herman Haupt
44th C.S. Maj. Gen. Jones M. Withers
48th U.S. Brig. Gen. Marsena E. Patrick
53rd U.S. Brig. Gen. Benjamin S. Roberts

1836 (49)

3rd C.S. Brig. Gen. Danville Leadbetter
4th C.S. Brig. Gen. Joseph R. Anderson
5th U.S. Brig. Gen. Montgomery C. Meigs
6th U.S. Brig. Gen. Daniel P. Woodbury
18th U.S. Brig. Gen. Thomas W. Sherman
22nd U.S. Brig. Gen. Henry H. Lockwood
24th U.S. Brig. Gen. John W. Phelps
33rd U.S. Brig. Gen. Robert Allen
46th C.S. Brig. Gen. Lloyd Tilghman

1837 (50)

1st U.S. Brig. Gen. Henry W. Benham
5th C.S. Gen. Braxton Bragg
6th U.S. Brig. Gen. Alexander B. Dyer
8th C.S. Brig. Gen. William W. Mackall
9th U.S. Brig. Gen. Eliakim Parker Scammon
10th U.S. Brig. Gen. Lewis G. Arnold
11th U.S. Brig. Gen. Israel Vogdes
12th U.S. Brig. Gen. Thomas Williams

18th C.S. Lt. Gen. Jubal A. Early
22nd U.S. Maj. Gen. William H. French
24th U.S. Maj. Gen. John Sedgwick
27th C.S. Lt. Gen. John Pemberton
29th U.S. Maj. Gen. Joseph Hooker
33rd C.S. Maj. Gen. Arnold Elzey [Jones]
39th U.S. Brig. Gen. John B. S. Todd
46th C.S. Maj. Gen. William H. T. Walker
48th C.S. Brig. Gen. Robert H. Chilton
*c C.S. Brig. Gen. Lewis A. Armistead
*a C.S. Brig. Gen. St. John R. Liddell

1838 (45)

2nd C.S. Gen. Pierre G.T. Beauregard
3rd C.S. Brig. Gen. James H. Trapier
17th U.S. Brig. Gen. William F. Barry
23rd U.S. Maj. Gen. Irvin McDowell
26th C.S. Lt. Gen. William J. Hardee
29th U.S. Brig. Gen. Robert S. Granger
31st C.S. Brig. Gen. Henry Hopkins Sibley
32nd C.S. Maj. Gen. Edward Johnson
35th C.S. Brig. Gen. Alexander W. Reynolds
36th U.S. Maj. Gen. Andrew Jackson Smith
40th U.S. Brig. Gen. Justus McKinstry
42nd C.S. Maj. Gen. Carter L. Stevenson

1839 (31)

1st U.S. Maj. Gen. Isaac I. Stevens
3rd U.S. Maj. Gen. Henry Halleck
4th C.S. Maj. Gen. Jeremy F. Gilmer
10th U.S. Brig. Gen. Joseph A. Haskin
13th C.S. Brig. Gen. Alexander R. Lawton
16th U.S. Brig. Gen. James B. Ricketts
17th U.S. Maj. Gen. Edward O. C. Ord

19th U.S. Brig. Gen. Henry J. Hunt
24th U.S. Brig. Gen. Eleazer A. Paine
30th U.S. Maj. Gen. Edward R.S. Canby
*c U.S. Brig. Gen. Gustavus A. DeRussy
*c U.S. Brig. Gen. John C. Robinson
*a U.S. Brig. Gen. Andrew Porter

1840 (42)

1st C.S. Brig. Gen. Paul O. Hebert
6th U.S. Maj. Gen. William Tecumseh Sherman
9th U.S. Brig. Gen. Stewart Van Vliet
10th C.S. Maj. Gen. John P. McCown
12th U.S. Maj. Gen. George H. Thomas
13th C.S. Lt. Gen. Richard S. Ewell
14th C.S. Brig. Gen. James G. Martin
15th U.S. Brig. Gen. George W. Getty
18th U.S. Brig. Gen. William Hays
23rd C.S. Brig. Gen. Bushrod R. Johnson
31st C.S. Brig. Gen. William Steele
41st C.S. Brig. Gen. Thomas Jordan

1841 (52)

1st U.S. Brig. Gen. Zealous B. Tower
2nd U.S. Maj. Gen. Horatio G. Wright
5th U.S. Brig. Gen. Amiel W. Whipple
[7th U.S. Col. Thomas J. Rodman, artillery expert]
8th U.S. Brig. Gen. Albion P. Howe
11th U.S. Brig. Gen. Nathaniel Lyon
19th C.S. Maj. Gen. Samuel Jones
22nd U.S. Brig. Gen. Joseph B. Plummer
23rd U.S. Brig. Gen. John M. Brannan
24th U.S. Maj. Gen. Schuyler Hamilton
26th U.S. Maj. Gen. John F. Reynolds
27th C.S. Brig. Gen. Robert S. Garnett
29th C.S. Brig. Gen. Richard B. Garnett
32nd U.S. Maj. Gen. Don Carlos Buell

34th U.S. Brig. Gen. Alfred Sully
38th U.S. Maj. Gen. Israel B. Richardson
39th C.S. Brig. Gen. John Marshall Jones
41st C.S. Brig. Gen. Claudius W. Sears
46th U.S. Maj. Gen. William T.H. Brooks
51st C.S. Brig. Gen. Abraham Buford

1842 (56)

1st U.S. Brig. Gen. Henry L. Eustis
2nd U.S. Maj. Gen. John Newton
5th U.S. Maj. Gen. John S. Rosecrans
8th C.S. Brig. Gen. Gustavus W. Smith
9th C.S. Maj. Gen. Mansfield Lovell
16th C.S. Maj. Gen. Martin Luther Smith
17th U.S. Maj. Gen. John Pope
23rd U.S. Brig. Gen. Seth Williams
24th U.S. Maj. Gen. Abner Doubleday
28th C.S. Lt. Gen. Daniel H. Hill
29th U.S. Maj. Gen. Napoleon J. T. Dana
39th U.S. Maj. Gen. George Sykes
40th C.S. Lt. Gen. Richard H. Anderson
48th C.S. Maj. Gen. Lafayette McLaws
52nd C.S. Maj. Gen. Earl Van Dorn
54th C.S. Lt. Gen. James Longstreet
*c C.S. Brig. Gen. James Monroe Goggin

1843 (39)

1st U.S. Maj. Gen. William B. Franklin
6th U.S. Brig. Gen. Isaac F. Quinby
7th C.S. Brig. Gen. Roswell S. Ripley
8th U.S. Maj. Gen. John J. Peck
10th U.S. Maj. Gen. Joseph J. Reynolds
11th U.S. Brig. Gen. James A. Hardie
14th C.S. Maj. Gen. Samuel G. French
16th U.S. Maj. Gen. Christopher C. Augur
17th C.S. Maj. Gen. Franklin Gardner

21st U.S. Lt. Gen. Ulysses S. Grant
22nd U.S. Brig. Gen. Joseph H. Potter
26th U.S. Brig. Gen. Charles S. Hamilton
30th U.S. Maj. Gen. Frederick Steele
32nd U.S. Brig. Gen. Rufus Ingalls
33rd U.S. Brig. Gen. Frederick T. Dent
35th U.S. Brig. Gen. Henry Moses Judah
*a U.S. Brig. Gen. Nelson G. Williams

1844 (25)

4th C.S. Brig. Gen. Daniel M. Frost
7th U.S. Maj. Gen. Alfred Pleasonton
11th C.S. Lt. Gen. Simon Bolivar Buckner
18th U.S. Maj. Gen. Winfield Scott Hancock
20th U.S. Brig. Gen. Alexander Hays

1845 (41)

1st C.S. Maj. Gen. William H. C. Whiting
3rd C.S. Brig. Gen. Louis Hebert
4th U.S. Maj. Gen. William F. Smith
7th U.S. Brig. Gen. Charles P. Stone
8th U.S. Maj. Gen. Fitz John Porter
17th U.S. Brig. Gen. John P. Hatch
25th C.S. Gen. Edmund Kirby Smith
27th U.S. Brig. Gen. John W. Davidson
33rd C.S. Brig. Gen. Barnard E. Bee
35th U.S. Maj. Gen. Gordon Granger
38th U.S. Brig. Gen. David A. Russell
40th U.S. Brig. Gen. Thomas G. Pitcher
*c U.S. Brig. Gen. Washington L. Elliott
*c U.S. Brig. Gen. George W. Morgan

1846 (59)

2nd U.S. Maj. Gen. George B. McClellan
4th U.S. Maj. Gen. John G. Foster
8th U.S. Maj. Gen. Jesse L. Reno

13th U.S. Maj. Gen. Darius N. Couch
17th C.S. Lt. Gen. Thomas J. Jackson
19th U.S. Brig. Gen. Truman Seymour
21st U.S. Brig. Gen. Charles C. Gilbert
32nd U.S. Brig. Gen. Samuel D. Sturgis
33rd U.S. Maj. Gen. George Stoneman
35th C.S. Brig. Gen. William D. Smith
37th C.S. Maj. Gen. Dabney H. Maury
38th U.S. Brig. Gen. Innis N. Palmer
41st C.S. Maj. Gen. David R. Jones
43rd U.S. Brig. Gen. George H. Gordon
45th U.S. Brig. Gen. Alfred Gibbs
54th C.S. Maj. Gen. Cadmus M. Wilcox
55th C.S. Brig. Gen. William M. Gardner
58th C.S. Brig. Gen. Samuel Bell Maxey
59th C.S. Maj. Gen. George E. Pickett
*c C.S. Brig. Gen. Birkett D. Fry

1847 (38)

8th U.S. Brig. Gen. Orlando B. Willcox
9th U.S. Brig. Gen. John S. Mason
14th U.S. Brig. Gen. James B. Fry
15th C.S. Lt. Gen. Ambrose P. Hill
18th U.S. Maj. Gen. Ambrose E. Burnside
20th U.S. Maj. Gen. John Gibbon
22nd U.S. Brig. Gen. Romeyn B. Ayres
23rd U.S. Maj. Gen. Charles Griffin
27th U.S. Brig. Gen. Thomas H. Neill
28th U.S. Brig. Gen. William W. Burns
30th U.S. Brig. Gen. Ebgert L. Viele
33rd U.S. Brig.Gen. Lewis C. Hunt
37th C.S. Brig. Gen. George H. Steuart
38th C.S. Maj. Gen. Henry Heth

1848 (38)

4th C.S. Brig. Gen. Walter H. Stevens

10th C.S. Brig. Gen. William E. Jones
16th U.S. Brig. Gen. John Buford
30th C.S. Brig. Gen. William N. R. Beall
36th C.S. Brig. Gen. Nathan G. Evans
*d U.S. Brig. Gen. Hugh B. Ewing

1849 (43)

1st U.S. Maj. Gen. Quincy A. Gillmore
2nd U.S. Maj. Gen. John G. Parke
5th C.S. Brig. Gen. Johnson K. Duncan
9th U.S. Brig. Gen. Absalom Baird
17th C.S. Brig. Gen. John C. Moore
18th U.S. Brig. Gen. Rufus Saxton
25th C.S. Brig. Gen. Beverly H. Robertson
27th C.S. Maj. Gen. Charles W. Field
28th C.S. Brig. Gen. Seth Maxwell Barton
30th U.S. Brig. Gen. Richard W Johnson
34th C.S. Brig. Gen. John W. Frazer
43rd C.S. Brig. Gen. James McQ. McIntosh

1850 (44)

2nd U.S. Maj. Gen. Gouverneur K. Warren
4th U.S. Brig. Gen. Cuvier Grover
12th U.S. Brig. Gen. Adam J. Slemmer
13th U.S. Brig. Gen. Richard Arnold
15th C.S. Brig. Gen. Lucius M. Walker
17th C.S. Brig. Gen. Armistead L. Long
18th C.S. Maj. Gen. Robert Ransom, Jr.
19th U.S. Brig. Gen. Eugene A. Carr
20th U.S. Brig. Gen. William P. Carlin
22nd C.S. Brig. Gen. Charles S. Winder
33rd C.S. Brig. Gen. William L. Cabell
38th C.S. Brig. Gen. Jean J. A. A. Mouton

1851 (42)

1st U.S. Brig. Gen. George L. Andrews

2nd U.S. Brig. Gen. James St. Clair Morton
8th U.S. Brig. Gen. Kenner Garrard
9th C.S. Brig. Gen. Benjamin H. Helm
11th U.S. Brig. Gen. Alvan C. Gillem
13th U.S. Brig. Gen. William D. Whipple
27th U.S. Brig. Gen. William H. Morris
33rd C.S. Brig. Gen. Junius Daniel
42nd C.S. Brig. Gen. Lawrence S. Baker
*c U.S. Brig. Gen. Marcellus M. Crocker

1852 (43)

7th U.S. Maj. Gen. Henry W. Slocum
8th U.S. Maj. Gen. David S. Stanley
10th C.S. Brig. Gen. George B. Anderson
14th U.S. Brig. Gen. Milo S. Hascall
17th C.S. Brig. Gen. George B. Cosby
20th U.S. Maj. Gen. Charles R. Woods
22nd C.S. Maj. Gen. John H. Forney
30th U.S. Maj. Gen. Alexander McD. McCook
35th U.S. Brig. Gen. August V. Kautz
38th U.S. Maj. Gen. George Crook
40th U.S. Brig. Gen. John P. Hawkins

1853 (52)

1st U.S. Maj. Gen. James B. McPherson
3rd U.S. Brig. Gen. Joshua W. Sill
4th C.S. Brig. Gen. William R. Boggs
6th U.S. Brig. Gen. William Sooy Smith
7th U.S. Maj. Gen. John McA. Schofield
13th C.S. Maj. Gen. John S. Bowen
16th U.S. Brig. Gen. William R. Terrill
22nd U.S. Brig. Gen. Robert O. Tyler
31st C.S. Brig. Gen. John R. Chambliss, Jr.
33rd C.S. Brig. Gen. Henry B. Davidson
34th U.S. Maj. Gen. Philip H. Sheridan
41st C.S. Brig. Gen. Henry H. Walker

43rd U.S. Brig. Gen. Alexander Chambers
44th C.S. Gen. John Bell Hood
45th C.S. Brig. Gen. James A. Smith
*c U.S. Brig. Gen. Davis Tillson
*b U.S. Brig. Gen. William Dwight

1854 (46)

1st C.S. Maj. Gen. George W. C. Lee
3rd U.S. Brig. Gen. Thomas H. Ruger
4th U.S. Maj. Gen. Oliver O. Howard
7th C.S. Brig. Gen. James Deshler
10th C.S. Brig. Gen. John Pegram
13th C.S. Maj. Gen. J. E. B. Stuart
14th C.S. Brig. Gen. Archibald Gracie, Jr.
17th C.S. Lt. Gen. Stephen D. Lee
19th C.S. Maj. Gen. William D. Pender
22nd C.S. Brig. Gen. John B. Villepigue
27th U.S. Brig. Gen. Stephen H. Weed

1855 (34)

2nd U.S. Maj. Gen. Godfrey Weitzel
6th U.S. Brig. Gen. David McM. Gregg
12th C.S. Brig. Gen. Francis R. T. Nicholls
13th U.S. Brig. Gen. Alexander S. Webb
14th U.S. Brig. Gen. John W. Turner
21st U.S. Brig. Gen. Alfred T. A. Torbert
26th U.S. Brig. Gen. William W. Averell
28th U.S. Brig. Gen. William B. Hazen
[*c James A. Whistler, of "Whistler's Mother"]

1856 (49)

6th U.S. Brig. Gen. Orlando M. Poe
10th U.S. Brig. Gen. Francis L. Vinton
11th U.S. Brig. Gen. George D. Bayard
19th C.S. Brig. Gen. Hylan B. Lyon
21st C.S. Maj. Gen. Lunsford Lindsay Lomax

23rd C.S. Brig. Gen. James P. Major
28th U.S. Brig. Gen. James W. Forsyth
38th C.S. Brig. Gen. William H. Jackson
41st U.S. Brig. Gen. William P. Sanders
44th U.S. Brig. Gen. Samuel S. Carroll
45th C.S. Lt. Gen. Fitzhugh Lee
*c C.S. Brig. Gen. William W. Kirkland

1857 (38)

3rd C.S. Brig. Gen. Edward P. Alexander
5th U.S. Brig. Gen. George C. Strong
12th U.S. Brig. Gen. Charles H. Morgan
19th C.S. Brig. Gen. Samuel W. Ferguson
30th C.S. Maj. Gen. John S. Marmaduke
35th C.S. Brig. Gen. Robert H. Anderson
*b U.S. Brig. Gen. John M. Corse

1858 (27)

16th U.S. Brig. Gen. Charles G. Harker
22nd C.S. Brig. Gen. Bryan M. Thomas

1859 (22)

11th U.S. Brig. Gen. Martin D. Hardin
17th U.S. Brig. Gen. Edwin H. Stoughton
19th C.S. Maj. Gen. Joseph Wheeler

1860 (41)

6th U.S. Maj. Gen. James H. Wilson
14th C.S. Maj. Gen. Stephen D. Ramseur
22nd U.S. Maj. Gen. Wesley Merritt
40th U.S. Brig. Gen. James M. Warner

1861, May Graduation (45)

5th U.S. Brig. Gen. Adelbert Ames
8th U.S. Brig. Gen. Emory Upton
10th U.S. Brig. Gen. Edmund Kirby

17th U.S. Maj. Gen. Judson Kilpatrick
*d C.S. Maj. Gen. Thomas L. Rosser
*d C.S. Brig. Gen. Pierce M. B. Young

1861, June Graduation (34)

34th U.S. Brig. Gen. George A. Custer
*d C.S. Brig. Gen. John H. Kelly
*d C.S. Brig. Gen. Felix H. Robertson

1862 (28)

1st U.S. Brig. Gen. Ranald S. Mackenzie
*c C.S. Brig. Gen. James Dearing

Seventeen West Point Drop-Outs
Who Became Generals in the Civil War

1. C.S. Brig. Gen. Benjamin G. Humphreys, ex-Class of '29
2. C.S. Brig. Gen. Lewis A. Armistead, ex-Class of '37
3. C.S. Brig. Gen. St. John R. Liddell, ex-Class of '37
4. U.S. Brig. Gen. Gustavus A. DeRussy, U.S. ex-Class of '39
5. U.S. Brig. Gen. Andrew Porter, ex-Class of '39
6. U.S. Brig. Gen. John C. Robinson, ex-Class of '39
7. C.S. Brig. Gen. James Monroe Goggin, ex-Class of '42
8. U.S. Brig. Gen. Nelson G. Williams, ex-Class of '43
9. U.S. Brig. Gen. Washington L. Elliott, ex-Class of '45
10. U.S. Brig. Gen. George W. Morgan, ex-Class of '45
11. C.S. Brig. Gen. Birkett D. Fry, ex-Class of '46
12. U.S. Brig. Gen. Hugh B. Ewing, ex-Class of '48
13. U.S. Brig. Gen. Marcellus M. Crocker, ex-Class of '51
14. U.S. Brig. Gen. William Dwight, ex-Class of '53
15. U.S. Brig. Gen. Davis Tillson, ex-Class of '53
16. C.S. Brig. Gen. William W. Kirkland, ex-Class of '56
17. U.S. Brig. Gen. John M. Corse, ex-Class of '57

Six Men Who Resigned from West Point in 1861 and Became Confederate Generals

1. James Dearing, ex-Class of '62
2. John H. Kelly, ex-Class of June '61
3. John Pelham, ex-Class of May '61 (Honorable Mention)
4. Felix H. Robertson, ex-Class of June '61
5. Thomas L. Rosser, ex-Class of May '61
6. Pierce M. B. Young, ex-Class of May '61

Robert E. Lee's Background

General Robert E. Lee's Ancestry

1. Richard Lee of Shropshire, Northumberland County, England, died 1644; married Anne Constable
2. Richard Lee (1646-1714) married Laetitia Corbin (1657-1706)
3. Henry Lee (1691-1747) married Mary Bland
4. Henry Lee (1729-1787) married Lucy Grimes
5. Henry ("Light Horse Harry") Lee (1756-1818) married secondly wife Ann Hill Carter
6. Robert Edward Lee (1807-1870) married Mary Anne Custis

Robert E. Lee's Marks at West Point

Category	Score
Rank	2/46
Mathematics	286/300
Natural Philosophy	295/300
Drawing	97/100
Engineering	292/300
Chemistry	99/100
Rhetoric & Moral Philosophy	199/200
French	98.5/100

Tactics	100/100
Conduct	300/300
General Merit	1966.5/2000

Foreign Born Generals

Foreign Born Confederate Generals

French

Maj. Gen. Camille Armand Jules Marie, Prince de Polignac
Brig. Gen. Xavier B. Debray
Brig. Gen. Pierre Soule

German

Brig. Gen. Robert Bechan
Brig. Gen. John A. Wagener

English

Brig. Gen. Collett Leventhorpe

Irish

Brig. Gen. William M. Browne
Maj. Gen. Patrick R. Cleburne
Brig. Gen. Joseph Finnegan
Brig. Gen. James Hagan
Brig. Gen. Patrick T. Moore
Brig. Gen. Walter P. Lane

Scottish

Brig. Gen. Peter Alexander
Brig. Gen. Selkirk McGlashan

Union Generals Who Were American Citizens Born Abroad

George G. Meade (Spain)
Jacob D. Cox (Canada)

Foreign Born Union Generals

German

Brig. Gen. Adolph Wilhelm August
Brig. Gen. Ludwig Blenker
Brig. Gen. Heinrich Bohlen
Brig. Gen. August V. Kautz
Brig. Gen. Karl Leopold Matthies
Maj. Gen. Peter J. Osterhaus
Brig. Gen. Friederich S. Salomon
Brig. Gen. Alexander von Schimmelfennig
Maj. Gen. Carl Schurz
Maj. Gen. Franz Sigel
Brig. Gen. Friederich, Baron von Steinwehr
Brig. Gen. Max von Weber
Brig. Gen. August von Villich

Russian

Brig. Gen. John Basil Turchin

Swedish

Brig. Gen. Charles J. Stohlbrand

Irish

Brig. Gen. Michael Corcoran
Brig. Gen. Thomas F. Meagher
Brig. Gen. Robert Patterson
Maj. Gen. Philip Sheridan
Brig. Gen. James Shields

Brig. Gen. Thomas A. Smyth
Brig. Gen. Thomas W. Sweeny

French

Brig. Gen. Alfred Nattie Duffie
Brig. Gen. Philippe Regis de Trobriand

Spanish

Brig. Gen. Edward Ferrero

Prewar Professions of Generals

Statistical Summary of the Prewar Profession of the Confederate Generals

Rank	Occupation	Number	% of Generals
1.	Law	129	30.4%
2.	Military	127	29.9%
2.	Army	125	29.4%
3.	Business	55	12.9%
4.	Agriculture	42	9.9%
5.	Politics	24	5.6%
6.	Education	15	3.5%
7.	Engineering	13	3.1%
8.	Other	6	1.4%
9.	Students	6	1.4%
10.	Medicine	4	0.9%
11.	Clergy	3	0.7%
12.	Journalism	1	0.2%
12.	Marines	1	0.2%
12.	Navy	1	0.2%
		425	

"Military" includes active Army, Navy, and Marines, plus cadets. Medicine includes pharmacy.

Statistical Summary of the Prewar Profession of the Union Generals

Rank	Occupation	Number	% of Generals
1.	Military	197	33.8%
1.	Army	194	33.3%
2.	Law	126	21.6%
3.	Business	116	19.9%
4.	Politics	47	8.1%
5.	Engineering	26	4.5%
6.	Agriculture	23	3.9%
7.	Education	16	2.7%
8.	Medicine	11	1.9%
9.	Students	8	1.4%
10.	Other	6	1.0%
11.	Journalism	6	1.0%
12.	Clergy	1	0.2%

"Military" includes active Army, Navy, and Marines, plus cadets.
Medicine includes pharmacy.

Twenty Generals With Very Unusual Civilian Occupations

1. U.S. Brig. Gen. George L. Beale, bookbinder.
2. U.S. Brig. Gen. Elon Farnsworth, wagoner
3. U.S. Brig. Gen. Edward Ferrero, dancing teacher
4. C.S. Lt. Gen. Nathan Bedford Forrest, slave trader
5. U.S. Brig. Gen. Benjamin H. Grierson, music teacher
6. U.S. Brig. Gen. Charles A. Heckman, conductor on what is now the Jersey Central Railroad.
7. C.S. Brig. Gen. Mark P. Lowery, bricklayer.
8. U.S. Brig. Gen. Thomas J. Lucas, watchmaker
9. U.S. Brig. Gen. George Francis McGinnis, hatter
10. U.S. Brig. Gen. John McNeil, hatter
11. U.S. Brig. Gen. Jasper A. Maltby, gunsmith.
12. U.S. Brig. Gen. Mahlon D. Mason, pharmacist

13. U.S. Brig. Gen. Charles L. Matthias, liquor salesman
14. U.S. Maj. Gen. Ormsby MacKnight Mitchell, astronomer
15. U.S. Brig. Gen. William H. Morris, editor of what would become *Town and Country Magazine.*
16. U.S. Brig. Gen. James Nagle, paper hanger
17. U.S. Brig. Gen. James S. Negley, horticulturalist
18. U.S. Brig. Gen. John M. Oliver, pharmacist
19. C.S. Brig. Gen. Gilbert Moxley Sorrel, bank clerk
20. U.S. Brig. Gen. Erastus B. Tyler, furrier

Nine Civil War Generals Who Were Physicians in Private Life

1. C.S. Maj. Gen. James P. Anderson
2. C.S. Brig. Gen. John Bratton
3. U.S. Maj. Gen. Samuel Crawford
4. U.S. Brig. Gen. James L. Kiernan
5. U.S. Brig. Gen. Nathan Kimball
6. C.S. Brig. Gen. Lucius B. Northrop
7. C.S. Brig. Gen. Jerome Bonaparte Robertson
8. U.S. Brig. Gen. Robert K. Scott
9. U.S. Brig. Gen. Edward A. Wild

Four Clergymen Who Became Generals

1. C.S. Brig. Gen. Mark. P. Lowry was a Baptist minister.
2. C.S. Lt. Gen. Leonidas Polk was the Episcopal Bishop of Louisiana.
3. C.S. Brig. Gen. William H. Pendleton was an Episcopal minister.
4. U.S. Brig. Gen. William A. Pile was a Methodist minister.

Two Confederate Generals Who Studied at Saumur, the French Cavalry School

1. Lt. Gen. William J. Hardee
2. Brig. Gen. James M. Hawes

Four Filibusters Who Became Generals in the Civil War

1. Confederate Brig. Gen. Allison Nelson held the same rank in Narcisco Lopez's expedition to Cuba in 1849-1851.
2. Union Brig. Gen. Isaac H. Duval had also been in Narcisco Lopez's expedition to Cuba in 1849-1851.
3. Confederate Brig. Gen. Robert C. Tyler had been an officer during William Walker's first Nicaraguan Expedition
4. Union Brig. Gen. Thomas A. Smith also served as an officer during William Walker's first Nicaraguan expedition.

One Union General Who Had Been Cashiered from the Army before the Civil War

1. Brig. Gen. William R. Montgomery

In 1855, Montgomery (U.S.M.A., '25), was dismissed from the Regular Army after it was discovered that he had been pocketing public moneys in his care. Normally such a disgrace would have barred him from military service thereafter, but he volunteered for active duty at the onset of the Civil War and proved capable enough to rise to a star.

Eight Naval Officers Who Became Union Generals

1. Brig. Gen. Samuel Powhatan Carter was a lieutenant in the Navy on the outbreak of the war, when he volunteered for the army: continuing in the Navy after the war, he retired as a rear admiral, thus becoming the only man in

American History to have been both a general and an admiral.

2. Brig. Gen. George Henry Chapman, a former midshipman, U.S.N., was assistant clerk of the House of Representatives when he volunteered in 1861.

3. Brig. Gen. Charles K. Graham, a former midshipman who saw service with the U.S.N. during the Mexican War, was working as an engineer in 1861, when he volunteered.

4. Brig. Gen. John B. McIntosh, a former midshipman who had seen active service in the War with Mexico, was a businessman in 1861 and promptly volunteered.

5. Maj. Gen. William Nelson was the seniormost lieutenant in the Navy when the war broke out and he volunteered for service, was commissioned a brigadier general and subsequently rose to major general before being murdered by Union Brig. Gen. Jefferson C. Davis.

6. Brig. Gen. John W. Revere, a grandson of Paul Revere, served in the Navy for 22 years, resigning as a lieutenant in 1850. In 1861 he briefly returned to the Navy, but was shortly commissioned a colonel in the volunteer army, and rose to brigadier general.

7. Brig. Gen. Jeremiah C. Sullivan had served as a midshipman during and after the Mexican War, resigning in 1854 to practice law in Indiana, and was commissioned a colonel in 1861.

8. Brig. Gen. George W. Taylor had served as a midshipman from 1827 to 1831, when he resigned to become a farmer, subsequently serving in the army in Mexico and reenlisting in 1861.

Three Naval Officers Who Became Confederate Generals

1. Edward Higgins spent 18 years (1836-1854) in the U.S. Navy, rising from midshipman to lieutenant, before resigning to enter the steamship business, volunteering for Confederate service in 1861 and eventually rising to brigadier general.

2. Richard L. Page joined the U.S. Navy as a midshipman in 1824 and resigned as a commander to "go South" in 1861,

being initially commissioned in the Confederate Navy, in which he rose to captain, before becoming a brigadier general in 1864.

3. George W. Randolph served as a midshipman, U.S.N., 1831-1837, later practicing law until he volunteered for Confederate service in 1861, rising to brigadier general.

One Marine Who Became a Confederate General

1. William Whedbee Kirkland, Lt., U.S.M.C., 1855-1860, was appointed a captain in the Confederate Army in 1861 and by August of 1863 had been promoted to brigadier general.

All In the Family: Civil War Generals Who Were Kin

A surprising number of Civil War flag officers—generals, commodores, and admirals—were related in various ways, whether by blood or marriage.

Eleven Generals Related to the Lees of Virginia

1. C.S. Gen. Robert E. Lee.
2. C.S. Maj. Gen. George Washington Lee, his son.
3. C.S. Maj. Gen. William Henry Fitzhugh Lee, another son.
4. C.S. Lt. Gen. Fitzhugh Lee, a nephew.
5. U.S. Rear Adm. Samuel P. Lee, their cousin.
6. C.S. Gen. Samuel Cooper, Fitzhugh Lee's father-in-law.

7. U.S. Brig. Gen. Frank Wheaton was also Samuel Cooper's son-in-law, and hence a brother-in-law of Fitzhugh Lee.
8. C.S. Brig. Gen. James Terrill was a cousin to the Lees.
9. James Terrill's brother U.S. Brig. Gen. William R. Terrill served against his cousins side in the war.
10. C.S. Brig. Gen. Richard L. Page, son of Robert E. Lee's maternal aunt, and hence a cousin.
11. U.S. Brig. Gen. Frank Wheaton was also a son-in-law of Samuel Cooper, and hence a brother-in-law of Fitzhugh Lee.

Five Families with Four General Officers in the War

1. The Ewings: Brig. Gen. Hugh B. Ewing, his brothers Thomas Ewing, Jr., and Brig. Gen. Charles Ewing, and their foster-brother and brother-in-law Maj. Gen. William T. Sherman, all in Union service
2. The Jackson/Morison Connection: Brig. Gen. Rufus Barringer, Lt. Gen. D.H. Hill, and Lt. Gen. Thomas J. "Stonewall" Jackson were at one time or another all married to daughters of one Dr. R.H. Morison, who had yet another daughter who married Jefferson Davis, Confederates all, as was "Stonewall's" cousin Maj. Gen. William L. "Mudwall" Jackson.
3. The McCooks: Maj. Gen. Alexander McDowell McCook, his brothers Brig. Gen. Daniel McCook, Jr. and Brig. Gen. Robert L. McCook and their cousin Brig. Gen. Edward M. McCook, Yankees all, as were 14 of their less exalted other kinfolk.
4. The Porters: Union Maj. Gen. Fitz John Porter was the cousin of Rear Adm. David Dixon Porter and his brother Commodore William Dixon Porter, who were the foster-brothers of Adm. David Glasgow Farragut.
5. The Taylors: Union Brig. Gen. Joseph P. Taylor was the uncle of Confederate Lt. Gen. Richard Taylor, son of the late President Zachary Taylor, who was the brother-in-law of Confederate Brig. Gen. Allen Thomas, and of Jefferson Davis by his first marriage, while the Confederate Maj.

Gen. Lafayette McLaws was a nephew through marriage of the late president, and hence a cousin of Dick Taylor.

Eight Families with Three General Officers in the War

1. The Birney/Marshal Tie: Union Brig. Gen. William Birney and his brother Brig. Gen. David Bell Birney were cousins of Confederate Brig. Gen. Humphrey Marshal.
2. The Bufords: Brig. Gen. Napoleon Bonaparte Buford and his half-brother Brig. Gen. John Buford, in Union service, plus their Rebel cousin Brig. Gen. Abraham Buford.
3. The Cookes: Union Brig. Gen. Philip St. George Cooke plus his son Brig. Gen. John Rogers Cooke and his son-in-law, Lt. Gen. J.E.B. Stuart, both in Confederate service.
4. The Crittendens: Confederate Maj. Gen. George B. Crittenden, plus his brother Brig. Gen. Thomas L. Crittenden and their cousin Brig. Gen. Thomas T. Crittenden, both Yankees.
5. The Heberts: Confederate Brig. Gen. Walter H. Stevens was married to a sister of Brig. Gen. Louis Hebert, who was the cousin of Brig. Gen. Paul O. Hebert.
6. The Hunts: Brig. Gen. Henry J. Hunt and his brother Lewis C. Hunt, plus Lewis' father-in-law, Maj. Gen. Silas Casey, all in Union service.
7. The McCulloch/Govan Tie: Ben McCulloch, his brother Henry E. McCulloch, and their cousin Daniel C. Govan were all Confederate brigadiers.
8. The Morgan Connection: Confederate Brig. Gen. Basil W. Duke and Lt. Gen. A.P. Hill were married to sister of Confederate Brig. Gen. John H. Morgan.

Thirty-Nine Families with Two General Officers in the War

1. The Alexander/Lawton Link: Confederate Brig. Gen. E. P. Alexander was the brother-in-law of Confederate Brig. Gen. Alexander R. Lawton

2. The Armstrong/Walker Tie: Confederate brigadiers Frank C. Armstrong and Lucius M. Walker were brothers-in-law.

3. The Beall/Fagan Connection: Brig. Gen. W. N. R. Beall was the brother-in-law of Maj. Gen. James F. Fagan, both Confederates.

4. The Bees: Bernard E. Bee and his older brother Hamilton P. Bee were both Rebel brigadiers.

5. The Canby/Hawkins Connection: Union Maj. Gen. Edward R. S. Canby and his brother-in-law Brig. Gen. John P. Hawkins.

6. The Chestnut/Deas Link: Both James Chestnut, Jr., and his cousin Zachariah C. Deas were Confederate brigadier generals

7. The Cobbs: Howell Cobb and his brother Thomas R. R. Cobb were both Confederate brigadiers.

8. The Davies: Union Brig. Gen. Thomas A. Davies and his nephew Maj. Gen. Henry E. Davies.

9. The Fessendens: Union Brig. Gen. James D. Fessenden and his brother Maj. Gen. Francis Fessenden, the sons of William Pitt Fessenden, a sometime senator and Lincoln's Secretary of the Treasury.

10. The Forneys: Brig. Gen. William H. Forney was the older brother of Maj. Gen. John H. Forney, both in Confederate service.

11. The Garnetts: Confederate Brig. Gen. Robert S. Garnett, the first general to die in the war, was the cousin of Confederate Brig. Gen. Richard B. Garnett, who died leading a brigade during "Pickett's Charge."

12. The Garrards: Kenner Garrard and his cousin Theophilus T. Garrard were both Yankee brigadiers.

13. The Gordons: Confederate Maj. Gen. John B. Gordon was a distant cousin of Confederate Brig. Gen. James B. Gordon.

14. The Green/Major Tie: Thomas Green had been the brother-in-law of James P. Major, both Confederate brigadiers.

15. The Hardee/Kirkland Connection: Lt. Gen. William J. Hardee was the uncle by marriage of Brig. Gen. William W. Kirkland, both Confederates.

16. The Harrisons: the brothers James E. and Thomas Harrison were both Confederate brigadier generals.

17. The Hoveys: Brig. Gen. Alvin P. Hovey and his cousin Brig. Gen. Charles E. Hovey, both Yankees.

18. The Kirbys: Union Brig. Gen. Edmund Kirby and his cousin Confederate Gen. Edmund Kirby Smith.

19. The McIntoshes: Union Brig. Gen. John B. McIntosh and his brother Confederate Brig. Gen. James M. McIntosh.

20. The McClellan/Marcy Connection: Union Maj. Gen. George B. McClellan was the son-in-law of Union Brig. Gen. Randolph B. Marcy.

21. The Mackall/Sorrel Link: William W. Mackall and his brother-in-law Gilbert Moxley Sorrel were Confederate brigadiers.

22. The Meade/Wise Tie: Union Maj. Gen. George Meade's sister was married to Confederate Brig. Gen. Henry A. Wise.

23. The Paines: Union Brig. Gen. Eleazer A. Paine and his cousin Brig. Gen. Halbert Eleazer Paine

24. The Patterson/Abercrombie Link: Francis E. Patterson and his brother-in-law John J. Abercrombie were both Union brigadiers, moreover, Patterson's father was Maj. Gen. of Pennsylvania Militia Robert Patterson, who failed to detain Confederate forces in western Virginia during the Bull Run Campaign, there were arguably three Civil War generals in the family.

25. The Pendleton/Lee Connection: Both William N. Pendleton and his son-in-law Edwin G. Lee were Confederate brigadiers.

26. The Polks: Lt. Gen. Leonidas K. Polk was the uncle of Brig. Gen. Lucius E. Polk, both in Confederate service.

27. The Preston/Hampton Tie: Confederate Brig. Gen. John S. Preston was a half-uncle by marriage and father-in-law of Lt. Gen. Wade Hampton.

28. The Ransoms: Brig. Gen. Matt W. Ransom and his younger brother Maj. Gen. Robert Ransom, Jr., were both Confederates.

29. The Rices: Union Brig. Gen. Americus Samuel A. Rice was the older brother of Brig. Gen. Elliot W. Rice, also a Yankee.

30. The Ripleys: Union Brig. Gen. James W. Ripley was the Uncle of Confederate Brig. Gen. Roswell S. Ripley.

31. The Robertson's: Jerome Bonaparte Robertson and his son Felix H. Robertson were both Rebel brigadier generals.
32. The Sheridan/Rucker Tie: Union Maj. Gen. Phil Sheridan was the son-in-law of Union Brig. Gen. Daniel H. Rucker.
33. The Sibleys: Union Brig. Gen. Henry Hastings Sibley was a cousin of Confederate Brig. Gen. Henry Hopkins Sibley.
34. The Smiths: Union Brig. Gen. Morgan L. Smith was the elder brother of Union Brig. Gen. Giles A. Smith.
35. The Starkes: Brothers William E. Starke and Peter B. Starke were both Confederate brigadiers.
37. The Toombs/DuBose Connection: Both Robert Toombs and his son-in-law Dudley McIver DuBose were Rebel brigadiers.
38. The Wood/Helm Tie: Union Brig. Gen. John Wood was a second-cousin of Confederate Brig. Gen. Benjamin H. Helm, who was married to Mary Todd Lincoln's half-sister.
39. The Woods: Union Brig. Gen. Charles R. Woods was the younger brother of Union Brig. Gen. William B. Woods

The Best and Worst Generals

Ten Best Confederate Generals

1. Nathan B. Forrest
2. Robert E. Lee
3. Patrick R. Cleburne
4. Thomas J. Jackson
5. James Longstreet
6. A.P. Hill
7. J.E.B Stuart
8. John B. Hood (1862-1863)
9. D.H. Hill
10. William J. Hardee

Ten Worst Confederate Generals

1. W.H.C. Whiting
2. John B. Hood (1864)
3. David E. Twiggs
4. Benjamin Huger
5. William H. Carroll
6. Braxton Bragg
7. John B. Floyd
8. Gideon Pillow
9. P.G.T. Beauregard
10. Theophilus Holmes

Ten Best Union Generals

1. Ulysses S. Grant
2. Benjamin H. Grierson
3. George H. Thomas
4. William T. Sherman
5. Winfield S. Hancock
6. John A. Logan
7. Quincy Gillmore
8. Andrew A. Humphreys
9. James B. McPherson
10. John M. Schofield

Ten Worst Union Generals

1. Egbert B. Brown
2. John Pope
3. Samuel P. Heintzelman
4. John C. Fremont
5. George B. McClellan
6. Benjamin F. Butler
7. Louis Blenker
8. David Hunter

9. William S. Rosecrans

10. Ambrose E. Burnside

The Ten Worst Performances by a General on Either Side of the Civil War

1. C.S. Gen. John B. Hood at Nashville where he became the only man on either side to lose an entire army.
2. U.S. Maj. Gen. John Pope at Second Manassas during which he almost matched Hood's achievement.
3. U.S. Maj. Gen. Nathaniel P. Banks displayed distinguished incompetence in the Valley in 1862 and along the Red River in 1864.
4. C.S. Brig. Gen. Henry H. Sibley managed to miss every one of the battles fought by his troops during his failed New Mexico campaign.
5. C.S. Brig. Gen. John B. Floyd's exhibited extraordinary incompetence and cowardice at Fort Donelson.
6. C.S. Maj. Gen. Gideon Pillow's exhibited distinguished incompetence and cowardice at Fort Donelson.
7. U.S. Brig. Gen. Robert H. Milroy's failures in the Valley.
8. U.S. Maj. Gen. Ambrose Burnside's bloody repulse at Fredericksburg.
9. U.S. Brig. Gen. James H. Ledlie at The Crater during which he abandoned his division to shelter "in a bomb-proof ten rods to the rear of the line," whilst liberally partaking of whiskey.
10. U.S. Brig. Gen. Edward Ferrero, who also abandoned his division at The Crater, and shared a bottle with Ledlie.

The Dozen Most Successful Generals Who Had Absolutely No Military Experience Prior to the Civil War

Nearly a third of the 583 Union generals in the Civil War, 188 (32.3%) had no military experience whatsoever prior to the Civil War, as did more than a third of the 425 Confederate generals,

153 (36%). Some of these men were good, and some of them were bad. Forthwith, an alphabetical listing of those who were particularly successful.

1. C.S. Brig. Gen. Turner Ashby
2. U.S. Maj. Gen. Francis Barlow
3. U.S. Maj. Gen. Daniel Butterfield
4. U.S. Maj. Gen. Jacob D. Cox
5. C.S. Lt. Gen. Nathan B. Forrest
6. U.S. Maj. Gen. Benjamin H. Grierson
7. C.S. Maj. Gen. John B. Gordon
8. C.S. Lt. Gen. Wade Hampton
9. U.S. Maj. Gen. John A. Logan
10. U.S. Brig. Gen. Edward M. McCook
11. U.S. Maj. Gen. Nelson A. Miles
12. U.S. Maj. Gen. James S. Wadsworth

Age, Rank and Distribution

Average Age of the Civil War Generals in 1861

Confederate

Final Rank	Age
Brig. Gen.	36
Maj. Gen.	37
Lt. Gen.	41
Gen.	48
Overall	37

Union

Final Rank	Age
Brig. Gen.	37
Maj. Gen.	39

Lt. Gen.	38
Overall	37

One Union General Who Was Too Young to Vote

1. Brig. Gen. Galusha Pennypacker.
   Born 1 June 1844, Pennypacker was promoted brigadier general on 28 April 1865, 33 days before his 21st birthday, with seniority from 18 February, more than three months before his 21st birthday.

The Full Generals of the Confederate Army by Seniority

1. Samuel Cooper
2. Albert Sidney Johnston
3. Robert E. Lee
4. Joseph E. Johnston
5. Pierre G.T. Beauregard
6. Braxton Bragg
7. Edmund Kirby Smith, provisional rank
8. John Bell Hood, temporary rank, later reverting to lieutenant general.

General Officer Distribution by Rank

Confederate

Rank	Number	% of Generals
Brig. Gen.	328	77.2%
Maj. Gen.	72	16.9%
Lt. Gen.	17	4.0%
Gen.	8	1.9%
Total	**425**	

Union

Rank	Number	% of Generals
Brig. Gen.	450	77.2%
Maj. Gen.	132	22.6%
Lt. Gen.	1	0.2%
Total	**583**	

General Names

The Seven Most Improbably Named Generals of the War

1. C.S. Brig. Gen. States Rights Gist
2. U.S. Brig. Gen. Zealous B. Tower
3. U.S. Brig. Gen. Strong Vincent
4. C.S. Brig. Gen. Eppa Hunton
5. C.S. Brig. Gen. Bushrod Rust Johnson
6. U.S. Brig. Gen. Galusha Pennypacker
7. U.S. Brig. Gen. Jefferson C. Davis

The Generals Holding the Record for Longest Name

General	Letters
1. U.S. Brig. Gen. Alexander Schimmelfennig	
2. C.S. Maj. Gen. John C. Breckinridge	12
3. U.S. Maj. Gen. Samuel P. Heintzelman	11

Six Generals Named "George Washington"

1. U.S. Brig. Gen. George Washington Cullum
2. Brig. Gen. George Washington Deitzler

3. U.S. Brig. Gen. George Washington Getty
4. C.S. Brig. Gen. George Washington Gordon
5. C.S. Maj. Gen. George Washington Custis Lee
6. U.S. Brig. Gen. George Washington Morgan

Three Generals Named "Winfield Scott"

1. Union Maj. Gen. and Brevet Lt. Gen. Winfield Scott
2. Confederate Brig. Gen. Winfield Scott Featherstone
3. Union Maj. Gen. Winfield Scott Hancock

Honorable Mention: Lt. Winfield Scott Schley, U.S.N., later a Commodore, U.S.N., and one of the victors at Santiago in 1898.

The Thirteen Confederate Generals with the "Best" Nicknames

1. Lt. Gen. Thomas J. Jackson, "Stonewall," in reference to his steadiness under fire at First Bull Run, or "Old Blue Light," in reference to the odd glow in his eyes during battle, also "Old Jack" and "The Gallant Jackson."
2. Maj. Gen. William L. Jackson, Stonewall's cousin, who had to be content with "Mudwall."
3. Lt. Gen. Richard S. Ewell, "Baldy Dick."
4. Maj. Gen. John B. Magruder, "Prince John" in reference to his manner.
5. Brig. Gen. William E. Jones, "Grumble," due to his persistent griping.
6. Maj. Gen. Camille Armand Jules Marie, the Prince de Polignac, "Polecat," from the unpronounceability of his name on Southern lips.
7. Maj. Gen. David R. Jones, "Neighbor," from his friendly manner.
8. Lt. Gen. James Ewell Brown Stuart, "Beauty," his prewar tag, was replaced by the pedestrian "Jeb" after he grew a beard to hide his "girlish" chin.
9-10. Brig. Gen. George T. Anderson and Brig. Gen. William C.

Cabell were both known as "Tige," short for "Tiger," for their ferocity in action.

11. Brig. Gen. William Smith, called "Extra Billy" from his days in the stagecoach and express business.

12. Brig. Gen. Adam R. Johnson, known as "Stovepipe" he once used a couple of lengths of stovepipe mounted on some wagon wheels to bluff a considerably stronger Union force into retiring.

13. Maj. Gen. Edward Johnson, known as "Allegheny" or "Old Allegheny" from his Kentucky mountain home, was also often called "Old Clubby" because he was wont to lead his troops into battle waving a heavy old walking stick rather than the more traditional sword.

The Thirteen Union Generals with the "Best" Nicknames

1. Maj. Gen. Benjamin Butler, "Spoons," from his alleged penchant for swiping the silver whilst on occupation duty in New Orleans, and "Beast" for alleged insults which he had inflicted upon the women of the town, both nicknames being conferred by the Confederacy.

2. Maj. Gen. Henry Halleck, "Old Wooden Head," which replaced his pre-war tag, "Old Brains," when he turned out to be less able a commander than his intellectual attainments had suggested.

3. Maj. Gen. George Thomas, who was probably the most-nicknamed general of the war, was known as "Old Slow Trot," inspired by his "slow but certain" manner of conducting operations, "Old Pap," because of his deep concern for the welfare of his troops, "The Rock of Chickamauga," because he held the line on that disastrous occasion, and "The Sledge of Nashville," for the way in which he smashed John B. Hood at the last place.

4. Maj. Gen. Judson Kilpatrick, "Kill Cavalry," for his penchant for getting his troops into very tight spots.

5. Maj. Gen. Nathaniel Banks, dubbed "Commissary Banks" by the Confederates, since his constant disasters proved a steady source of supply for them.

6. Maj. Gen. Abner Doubleday, "Forty-Eight Hours," because of his lack of alacrity in the conduct of operations.

7. Maj. Gen. George Sykes, "Tardy George," also had "the slows."

8. Maj. Gen. Ormsby MacKnight Mitchell, "Old Stars," being by profession a distinguished astronomer.

9. Maj. Gen. John C. Fremont, "The Pathfinder," due to his pre-war fame as an explorer in the west, albeit that he proved wholly unable to locate Stonewall Jackson in the Shenandoah Valley.

10. Brig. Gen. Ivan Vasilevich—or John B.—Turchin, "The Russian Thunderbolt," from his ethnic origin.

11. Maj. Gen. Philip Sheridan, "Little Phil," due to his diminutive stature.

12. Maj. Gen. Israel B. Richardson, known as "Fighting Dick" and "Greasy Dick" due to his personal habits.

13. Maj. Gen. Edwin Vose Sumner was nicknamed "Bull Head" because a musket ball is once alleged to have bounced off his head.

General Personal Traits

The Five Most Eccentric Confederate Generals

1. C.S. Brig. Gen. William Smith indulged in extremely odd behavior on the battlefield, once going into action wearing a beaver "stove-pipe" hat and wielding a blue cotton umbrella.

2. C.S. Lt. Gen. Thomas J. Jackson was a hypochondriac, was wont to suck on lemons during battles, often held up his right arm "to let the blood drain out," would frequently fall into a trance-like state, often talked to himself, and had numerous other eccentricities as well.

3. C.S. Lt. Gen. Richard S. Ewell was known to occasionally make noises like a bird for no particular reason and would often eat raw grain, pecking at it like a bird.

4. C.S. Lt. Gen. Ambrose P. Hill was hypochondriacal to the point that he was sometimes unfit for duty.
5. C.S. Maj. Gen. G.W. Smith had a nervous breakdown after the battle of Seven Pines.

Seven Generals Notorious as Womanizers

1. U.S. Brig. Gen. George A. Custer
2. U.S. Maj. Gen. Joseph Hooker
3. U.S. Maj. Gen. Judson Kilpatrick
4. U.S. Maj. Gen. James B. Steedman
5. U.S. Brig. Gen. Edwin H. Stoughton
6. U.S. Brig. Gen. Julius Stahel
7. C.S. Maj. Gen. Earl Van Dorn

Six Generals Who Were Teetotalers

1. C.S. Lt. Gen. Nathan Bedford Forrest
2. U.S. Maj. Gen. Oliver O. Howard
3. C.S. Lt. Gen. Thomas J. Jackson
4. C.S. Maj. Gen. Gideon J. Pillow
5. C.S. Lt. Gen. Leonidas K. Polk
6. U.S. Brig. Gen. Neal Dow who ran for president on the Prohibition ticket in 1880.

Six Generals Known as Heavy Drinkers

1. C.S. Maj. Gen. George B. Crittenden
2. C.S. Brig. Gen. Nathan Evans
3. U.S. Lt. Gen. Ulysses S. Grant
4. U.S. Maj. Gen. Joseph Hooker
5. C.S. Brig. Gen. Henry H. Sibley
6. U.S. Brig. Gen. James H. Ledlie

Generals Killed in Personal Encounters

Ten Confederate Generals Killed in "Personal Encounters"

1. Brig. Gen. William W. Adams, by newspaper editor John Martin, with whom he had a political quarrel, on 1 May 1888 in Mississippi.
2. Brig. Gen. William F. Brantley, murdered by an unknown assassin in Mississippi on 2 November 1870.
3. Brig. Gen. James H. Clanton, murdered on 27 September 1871 in Tennessee by a former Union officer with whom he had a quarrel.
4. Maj. Gen. Bryan Grimes, killed in North Carolina on 14 August 1880 by one William Porter, an assassin in the hire of some of the general's enemies.
5. Maj. Gen. Thomas C. Hindman, slain by an unknown hand in Arkansas on 28 September 1868.
6. Brig. Gen. St. John R. Liddell was killed by Lt. Col. Charles Jones, late of the 17th Louisiana, and the latter's two sons, aboard a steamboat on the Black River in Louisiana on 14 February 1870, after a quarrel.
7. Brig. Gen. William F. Tucker, murdered in Mississippi on 14 September 1881 by two hired killers employed by a personal enemy.
8. Maj. Gen. Earl Van Dorn, shot in the back in Tennessee on 7 May 1863, by one Dr. George B. Peters, the general having seduced the latter's young wife.
9. Brig. Gen. Lucius M. Walker, slain by Brig. Gen. John S. Marmaduke in a duel at sunrise on 4 July 1863 at Little Rock, Arkansas.
10. Maj. Gen. John A. Wharton, shot by Col. George W. Baylor, 6 April 1865, in Texas.

One "Also Ran"

1. Nathan Bedford Forrest, badly wounded on 14 June 1863 during an "altercation" at Columbia, Tennessee, with one of his officers, Lt. A. Willis Gould, who subsequently died of knife wounds inflicted by Forrest.

One US General Killed in a "Personal Encounter"

1. Maj. Gen. William Nelson, shot by Brig. Gen. Jefferson C. Davis in Kentucky on 29 September 1862, after having slapped the latter's face.

General Mounts

The Favorite Mounts of Eight Prominent Confederate Generals

1. Maj. Gen. Patrick Cleburne lost his Dixie at Perryville.
2. Lt. Gen. Nathan Bedford Forrest lost so many horses in combat that it's difficult to say which was his favorite, but King Philip at least managed to survive the war.
3. Lt. Gen. Richard S. Ewell's favorite mount was Rifle, "a flea bitten grey."
4. Lt. Gen. Fitzhugh Lee's Nellie Gray was killed at Opequon.
5. Gen. Robert E. Lee's Traveler, a big gray, is certainly the most famous horse of the war, but the general also rode Richmond, Lucy Long, Ajax, and a mount known only as The Roan.
6. Lt. Gen. Thomas J. Jackson's favorite steed was "Old Sorrel" or "Little Sorrel," a small, ugly, inelegant mare to whom he was quite devoted, and on whom he was mounted at the time he was shot at Chancellorsville.
7. Gen. Albert Sidney Johnston was riding Fire-Eater, a

thoroughbred bay, at the time his was mortally wounded at Shiloh.

8. Lt. Gen. J.E.B. Stuart's favorite mount was Virginia, a remarkable thoroughbred mare who once enabled the general to escape pursuers by leaping an allegedly 15-foot wide ditch with several feet to spare. The general also regularly rode Highfly.

The Favorite Mounts of Nine Prominent Union Generals

1. Maj. Gen. Ben Butler usually rode Almond Eye.

2. Lt. Gen. Ulysses S. Grant's favorite horse was Cincinnati, which carried him from Chattanooga to Appomattox. His stable also included Jack, Fox, Kangaroo, and Jeff Davis.

3. Maj. Gen. Joseph Hooker's horse Lookout acquired his name at the Battle of Chattanooga.

4. Maj. Gen. Philip Kearny's Decatur was killed at Seven Pines. At the time of his death at Chantilly in September of 1862 Kearny was riding Bayard. His spare mount was Moscow.

5. Maj. Gen. George B. McClellan's favorite mount was Daniel Webster, a great bay beast whom he called "That devil Dan," but he also rode Burns, though only in the mornings, as the latter had the habit of bolting for the barn around dinner time.

6. Maj. Gen. George Meade, Baldy, a noble steed who was wounded twice at First Bull Run, and again at Antietam and Gettysburg, but managed to survive to walk in the general's funeral procession in 1878.

7. Maj. Gen. Philip Sheridan's favorite horse was Rienzi, who was sometimes called Winchester after the general's famous ride to the latter place during his Valley Campaign in '64. After his death, Rienzi was stuffed and can now be seen at the Smithsonian.

8. Maj. Gen. William T. Sherman's Sam was several times wounded under the general, but always recovered. Sherman's spare horse was Lexington.

9. Maj. Gen. George Thomas's favorite horse, Billy, named in honor of Thomas' good friend William T. Sherman, was

calm, unhurried, and deliberate, very much like his master.

The Five Generals Having the Most Mounts Killed Under Them

General	Horses Killed
1. C.S. Lt. Gen. Nathan Bedford Forrest	29
2. C.S. Maj. Gen. Joseph Wheeler	16
3. C.S. Brig. Gen. Alfred J. Vaughan, Jr.	8
4. C.S. Brig. Gen. William B. Bate,	6
5. U.S. Maj. Gen. William Tecumseh Sherman	5

Men Who Couldn't or Wouldn't be Generals

Four Men Who Didn't Want to be Generals

1. Henry Brown, a colonel in the Union Army, declined promotion to brigadier general on 28 September 1861.
2. Julius A. de Lagnel, a Confederate artilleryman, was offered a brigadier generalship to date from 15 April 1862, but declined the honor to serve as a lieutenant colonel in the Ordnance Bureau.
3. Thomas A. Morris was commissioned a Brigadier General of Indiana Volunteers in April of 1861, and in this capacity commanded a brigade in McClellan's West Virginia Campaign. His brigade was mustered out later that year, and he remained inactive thereafter. In September of 1862 he was offered a commission as Brigadier General of U.S. Volunteers but, apparently piqued at having been overlooked for so long, declined.
4. James St. Clair Morton, a Union engineer officer, voluntarily reverted to major shortly after Chickamauga, in late 1863,

after having served for nearly five months as a brigadier general of volunteers.

Three Distinguished Foreign Officers Who *Did Not* Become Union Generals During the Civil War

1. George Ernest Boulanger, who later muffed the chance to become military dictator of France through indecision, first clearly displayed this talent during the Civil War, when he began making inquiries about securing a commission in 1861 and was still making such in 1865.
2. Giuseppi Garibaldi, hero of the Uruguayan and Italian Revolutions, who was offered a corps in 1862, but declined because Lincoln was not at the time willing to declare immediate emancipation.
3. George Klapka, commander of the Hungarians during their Revolution of 1848-1849, whose terms were too stiff for Lincoln to accept (he wanted a salary of $100,000 a year).

One Confederate General Who Deserted

1. Brig. Gen. Daniel M. Frost.
   In late 1863 Frost, who served primarily as a staff officer, left for Canada, where his wife and family had fled to escape the war, without bothering to resign his commission or inform the Confederate War Department.

One Very Dead Man Who Became a Brevet General

1. William M. Graham.
   Lt. Col. Graham was given a brevet brigadier generacly on 13 March 1865, 6,396 days after he was killed in action at the head of the old *11th Infantry* at the battle of Molino del Rey, 8 August 1847.

General Appearances

Tonsorial Preferences of the Confederate Generals

Rank	Style	Number of Generals	% of Generals
1st	Bearded	285	67.1%
2nd	Mustachioed	77	18.1%
3rd	Clean Shaven	52	12.2%
4th	Muttonchopped	14	3.3%

Figures refer to the dominant style affected by the generals, granted that most bearded men would also be mustached.

Tonsorial Preferences of the Union Generals

Rank	Style	Number of Generals	% of Generals
1st	Bearded	391	67.1%
2nd	Mustachioed	101	17.3%
3rd	Muttonchopped	50	8.6%
4th	Clean Shaven	41	7.0%

Figures refer to the dominant style affected by the generals, granted that most bearded men would also be mustached.

Top 10 Strangest Hairstyles

1. U.S. Ambrose Burnside: probably the most famous sideburns in history.
2. C.S. Brig. Gen. Daniel Ruggles: the waterfall of whiskers.
3. C.S. Hiram Granbury: the Medusa.
4. C.S. Brig. Gen. Nathan George Evans: old scrubby.
5. U.S. Brig. Gen. John C. Robinson: a beard that reminds you of that curly mutt you had when you were a kid.

6. U.S. Maj. Gen. John M. Schofield: what he lacked on his head, he made up for on his chin.

7. C.S. Brig. Gen. William P. Hardeman: the blow dried look of the 1860s.

8. C.S. Brig. Gen. James B. Terrill: the scratch and sniff sideburns.

9. U.S. Maj. Gen. John Gray Foster: the old salt look.

10. U.S. Maj. Gen. Ulysses S. Grant early in the war: the long beard just doesn't look right somehow.

Ten Ugliest Generals

1. U.S. Maj. Gen. William T. Sherman
2. C.S. Lt. Gen. Nathan B. Forrest
3. U.S. Maj. Gen. Benjamin F. Butler
4. U.S. Maj. Gen. John A. McClernand
5. C.S. Brig. Gen. Nathan G. Evans
6. U.S. Maj. Gen. Henry W. Halleck
7. U.S. Maj. Gen. Philip H. Sheridan
8. U.S. Maj. Gen. Thomas W. Sherman
9. U.S. Maj. Gen. George G. Meade
10. C.S. Gen. Braxton Bragg

General General Data

Six Generals With Serious Prewar Physical Handicaps

1. U.S. Brig. Gen. Marcellus M. Crocker had consumption when he volunteered in 1861, and died from the disease a few weeks after the end of the war: Despite his condition, Crocker never missed a battle due to illness.

2. U.S. Brig. Gen. Joseph A. Haskin had lost his left arm at Chapultepec, in the War with Mexico, but remained on active duty.

3. C.S. Lt. Gen. Thomas J. Jackson was somewhat deaf in his left ear, and very much so in his right.

4. U.S. Maj. Gen. Philip Kearny had lost his left arm at Churubusco, in the War with Mexico. He resigned from the service in 1851, but volunteered for duty on the outbreak of the Civil War.

5. U.S. Brig. Gen. Thomas W. Sweeny lost his right arm at Churubusco. He remained in the Regular Army until he took command of Missouri volunteer troops after the outbreak of Civil War. Despite Sweeny's handicap, he started a fist fight with two fellow commanders after the battle of Atlanta.

6. C.S. Brig. Gen. James G. Martin lost his right arm at Churubusco, but remained on active duty, resigning to "go South" in 1861.

7. U.S. Brig. Davis Tillson lost one of his legs as a result of an accident in 1851, which caused him to resign from West Point in his third year: a decade later he volunteered for duty.

Three Generals Who Paid for Their Own Regiments

1. C.S. Lt. Gen. Bedford Forrest, raised a battalion of mounted infantry at his own expense.

2. C.S. Lt. Gen. Wade Hampton, financed Hampton's Legion.

3. U.S. Brig. Gen. James H. Van Allen, footed the bill.

Four Union Generals Who Made Balloon Ascents during the War

1. Maj. Gen. Benjamin Butler

2. Maj. Gen. George B. McClellan

3. Maj. Gen. Irvin McDowell

4. Maj. Gen. Fitz John Porter

Seven Union Generals from Galena, Illinois

1. Brig. Gen. Augusts L. Chetlain
2. Brig. Gen. John R. Duer
3. Lt. Gen. U.S Grant
4. Brig. Gen. Milo S. Hascall
5. Brig. Gen. Jasper A. Maltby
6. Brig. Gen. John A. Rawlins
7. Brig. Gen. John E. Smith

The apparent anomaly of so many senior officers coming from so small a town is best explained by looking at the third name on the list.

Five Union Generals
Distinguished as Grafters

1. Brig. Gen. La Fayette C. Baker who, in his capacity as special provost marshal for the War Department, was responsible for investigating graft, and in the process was not averse to picking up a little spare cash on the side.
2. Maj. Gen. Benjamin F. Butler, nicknamed "Spoons Butler" for his alleged light-fingeredness when about the property of persons sympathetic to the Rebels.
3. Brig. Gen. Justus McKinstry, who had been in charge of procurement for the Department of the West, became the only general, on either side to be cashiered for corruption, on 28 January 1863.
4. Brig. Gen. Robert K. Scott, who capped his career by becoming the "carpetbagger" governor of South Carolina, in which capacity he made a fraudulent issue of state bonds.
5. Brig. Gen. Francis Barretto Spinola, who resigned from the service in the face of a pending conviction by court martial for "conniving with bounty brokers to defraud and swindle recruits."

Three Union Generals Who Saw No Action against the Confederacy

1. Patrick E. Connor, earned a brigadier generacly fighting Plains Indians.
2. Henry Hastings Sibley also earned his star on the Plains.
3. George Wright spent the entire war in various administrative posts on the Pacific coast, being made a brigadier general in 1861.

Two Generals Who Killed Each Other

1. Union Brig. Gen. Theodore Read was slain in an exchange of pistol shots with Confederate Brig. Gen. James Dearing at High Bridge, Virginia, on 6 April 1865.
2. Confederate Brig. Gen. James Dearing was mortally wounded by Union Brig. Gen. Theodore Read in the same exchange of pistol shots at High Bridge, Virginia, on 6 April 1865 and died of his wounds on 23 April.

One Union General Who Was Also a Confederate Officer

1. Brig. Gen. Alfred T. A. Torbert.
   On 17 April 1861 Torbert, then a 1st Lieutenant in the U.S. Army was nominated and confirmed in the same rank by the Confederate Congress, at a time when he was mustering troops into Federal service in New Jersey. The most likely explanation for this unusual state of affairs is that whilst on leave during March of 1861, Torbert, a native of Delaware, may have toyed with the idea of joining the Confederacy and gone so far as to solicit a commission. Despite this, his services in the war were entirely satisfactory.

Six Unusual Books by Civil War Generals

1. *Swedenborg as a Hermetic Philospher* by U.S. Maj. Gen. Ethan Allen Hitchcock.
2. *Science as Witness to the Bible* by C.S. Brig. Gen. William Pendleton
3. *Bitumen* by U.S. Maj. Gen. Henry Halleck
4. *Plantation and Farm Instruction* by C.S. Brig. Gen. Philip St. George Cooke.
5. *A Digest of the Statute Laws of the State of Georgia* by C.S. Brig. Gen. Thomas R. R. Cobb.
6. *Ben Hur* by U.S. Maj. Gen. Lew Wallace

CHAPTER 6

TROOPS

Famous Firsts

Seven Unfortunate "Firsts" of the War

1. The first man killed: Union Pvt. Daniel Hough ["huff"] of *Company E, 1st Artillery*, due to the premature discharge of a cannon being used to fire a salute during evacuation ceremonies after the surrender of Fort Sumter.

2. The first man injured by hostile action: Nicholas Biddle, a Black freeman serving as an officer's orderly in *Company A, 27th Pennsylvania*, was struck and injured by a brick-bat thrown by some Southern sympathizers as the regiment paraded through Baltimore on 18 April 1861.

3. The first men to die by hostile action: Union Pvts. Sumner Needham, Luther C. Ladd, Addison O. Whitney. and Charles A. Taylor, of the *6th Massachusetts*, when the regiment was attacked by a secessionist mob as it marched through Baltimore on 19 April 1861, along with about a dozen of the rioters, who were shot down by the troops.

4. The first Regular Army officer killed: Union Lt. J. T. Greble of the *2nd Artillery*, who fell by his guns at Big Bethel on 10 June 1861.

5. The first Regular Army officer to be wounded: Union Capt.

Judson Kilpatrick of the *5th New York,* also at Big Bethel on 10 June 1861.
6. The first general killed: Confederate Brig. Gen. Robert S. Garnett, who fell on 13 July 1861, near Corrick's Ford, on the Cheat River in what is now West Virginia, to be followed by 123 other generals through April of 1865.
7. The first naval officer killed: Cdr. James H. Ward, U.S.N., on 27 June 1861, whilst leading an effort to dislodge some Confederate batteries covering the lower Potomac from Mathias Point, Virginia

Officers

The Officers of the Fort Sumter Garrison

1. Maj. Robert Anderson, later Maj. Gen., U.S.
2. Capt. Abner Doubleday, later Maj. Gen., U.S.
3. Capt. John G. Foster, later Maj. Gen., U.S.
4. Assistant Surgeon Samuel W. Crawford, later Maj. Gen., U.S.
5. 1st Lt. Jefferson C. Davis, later Brig. Gen., U.S.
6. 1st Lt. Truman Seymour, later Brig. Gen., U.S.
7. 1st Lt. G.W. Snyder, later colonel of volunteers
8. 2nd Lt. Norman J. Hall, later colonel of volunteers.
9. 2nd Lt. R.K. Meade, Jr., who later resigned to join the Confederacy, dying soon afterwards of natural causes.

Eight Notable Civil War Officers Who Took Part in the Wars for Italian Independence

1. Col. (and brevet Brig. Gen.) Luigi di Cesnola, served in the Italian War of 1848-1849 as a cavalry officer in the Sardinian Army, and afterwards founded the Metropolitan Museum of Art.
2. Union Brig. Gen. Gustave P. Cluseret was colonel of the

French volunteers fighting with Garibaldi at the Battle of the Volturno (1 October 1860).

3. Union Brig. Gen. Philip St. George Cooke, at the time colonel of the *2nd Dragoons* served in Italy as an official observer, 1859-1860.

4. Union Brig. Gen. Alfred Napoleon Alexander Duffie, was an officer with the French cavalry at Solferino (24 June 1859).

5. Union Maj. Gen. Philip Kearny, charged with the *Chasseurs d'Afrique* at Solferino (24 June 1859).

6. Union Volunteer aide-de-camp Robert d'Orleans, the *duc de Chartres*, and brother to the Bourbon pretender to the throne of France, had served as an officer with the Piedmontese Nizza Light Cavalry Regiment in 1859, earning a decoration for gallantry from, of all people, Napoleon III.

7. Confederate Maj. Gen. James J. Pettigrew was a volunteer observer with the Sardinian Army at San Martino (24 June 1859)

8. Confederate Lt. Col. Chatham R. Wheat, commander of the famed "Louisiana Tigers," served with Garibaldi's English volunteer legion in Sicily and Southern Italy, 1859-1860.

Union Army Officers Who Received the Thanks of Congress

Officer Action	Date
1. Nathaniel Lyon Wilson's Creek	24 December 1861
2. William S. Rosecrans Stones River	3 March 1863
3. Ulysses S. Grant "For Gallantry"	17 December 1863
4. Nathaniel P. Banks Port Hudson	28 January 1864
5. Ambrose E. Burnside "For Gallantry"	28 January 1864
6. Joseph Hooker "For the Defense of Washington and Maryland"	28 January 1864

7. George G. Meade Gettysburg	28 January 1864
8. Oliver O. Howard Gettysburg	28 January 1864
9. William T. Sherman Chattanooga	19 February 1864
10. Joseph Bailey Red River	11 June 1864
11. William T. Sherman Georgia	10 January 1865
12. Alfed H. Terry Fort Fisher	24 January 1865
13. Philip H. Sheridan Shenandoah Valley, 1864	9 February 1865
14. George H. Thomas Franklin and Nashville	3 March 1865
15. Winfield S. Hancock Gettysburg	21 April 1866
16. Newton M. Curtis Fort Fisher	

One Notable Illiterate Officer

1. Col. and Brevet Brig. Gen. Christopher "Kit" Carson, who was also probably the shortest notable officer in the war, standing less than 5'4".

Four Officers Who Left the Army in 1861 But *Did Not* Join the Confederacy

During the winter and Spring of 1860-1861 313 officers of the Regular Army resigned their commissions or were expelled from the service, fully 29% of the total. Most of these men soon afterwards joined the Confederacy. But not all.

1. 2nd Lt. James B. Alexander, resigned from the Regular Army, 9 May 1861, and died of natural causes shortly thereafter.
2. Capt. William B. Johns, "dropped" from the Regular Army,

11 April 1861 for being missing from his company without an explanation.
3. Capt. Henry S. Schroeder, resigned from the Regular Army, 30 May 1861.
4. Capt. William K. Van Boklelen, "cashiered" from the Regular Army, 8 May 1861 for "misapplication of $225 of public funds."

African American Soldiers

Highest Ranking Black Officers

Majors

Francis E. Dumas (*74th United States Colored Infantry*)
Martin R. Delany (*104th United States Colored Infantry*)

Captains

Alfred Bourgeau (*73rd United States Colored Infantry*)
Andre Calloux (*73rd United States Colored Infantry*)
Edward Carter (*73rd United States Colored Infantry*)
Edward C. Davis (*73rd United States Colored Infantry*)
John De Pass (*73rd United States Colored Infantry*)
Joseph Folin (*73rd United States Colored Infantry*)
James H. Ingraham (*73rd United States Colored Infantry*)
Alcide Lewis (*73rd United States Colored Infantry*)
James Lewis (*73rd United States Colored Infantry*)
Henry L. Rey (*73rd United States Colored Infantry*)
William B. Barrett (*74th United States Colored Infantry*)
William Belley (*74th United States Colored Infantry*)
Arnold Bertonneau (*74th United States Colored Infantry*)
Hannibal Carter (*74th United States Colored Infantry*)
Edward P. Chase (*74th United States Colored Infantry*)
Robert H. Isabelle (*74th United States Colored Infantry*)
P.B.S. Pinchback (*74th United States Colored Infantry*)

Samuel W. Ringgold (*74th United States Colored Infantry*)
Joseph Villeverde (*74th United States Colored Infantry*)
Samuel J. Wilkinson (*74th United States Colored Infantry*)
Leon G. Forstall (*75th United States Colored Infantry*)
Peter A. Gardener (*75th United States Colored Infantry*)
Charles W. Gibbons (*75th United States Colored Infantry*)
Jacques A. Gla (*75th United States Colored Infantry*)
John C. Holland (*75th United States Colored Infantry*)
Samuel Lawrence (*75th United States Colored Infantry*)
Joseph P. Oliver (*75th United States Colored Infantry*)
O.S.B. Wall (*104th United States Colored Infantry*)
H. Ford Douglas (*Independent Battery, United States Colored Light Artillery*)

Black Soldiers Who Won the Medal of Honor

Private William H. Barnes, *Co. C, 38th United States Colored Infantry*, at Chaffin's Farm, Virginia, 29 September 1864.

First Sergeant Powhatan Beaty, *Co. G, 5th United States Colored Infantry*, 29 September 1864.

Sergeant William H. Carney, *Co. C, 54th Massachusetts Colored Infantry*, at Fort Wagner, S.C., 18 July 1863.

Sergeant Decatur Dorsey, *Co. B, 39th United States Colored Infantry*, at Petersburg, Virginia, 30 July 1864.

Sergeant Major Christian A. Fleetwood, *4th United States Colored Infantry*, at Chaffin's Farm, Virginia, 29 September 1864.

Private James Gardiner, *Co. I, 36th United States Colored Infantry*, at Chaffin's Farm, Virginia, 29 September 1864.

Sergeant James H. Harris, *Co B, 38th United States Colored Infantry*, at New Market Heights, Virginia, 29 September 1864.

Sergeant Major Thomas Hawkins, *6th United States Colored Infantry*, at Deep Bottom, Virginia, 21 July 1864.

Sergeant Alfred B. Hilton, *Co. H, 4th United States Colored Infantry*, at Chaffin's Farm, Virginia, 29 September 1864.

Sergeant Milton M. Holland, *5th United States Colored Infantry*, at Chaffin's Farm, Virginia, 29 September 1864.

Corporal Miles James, *Co. B, 36th United States Colored Infantry,* at Chaffin's Farm, Virginia, 29 September 1864.

First Sergeant Alexander Kelly, *Co. F, 6th United States Colored Infantry,* at Chaffin's Farm, Virginia, 29 September 1864.

First Sergeant Robert Pinn, *Co. I, 5th United States Colored Infantry,* at Chaffin's Farm, Virginia, 29 September 1864.

Private Charles Veal, *Co. D, 4th United States Colored Infantry,* at Chaffin's Farm, Virginia, 29 September 1864.

Two Black Naval Heroes of the Civil War

1. Robert Smalls: a slave and harbor pilot, escaped from Charleston, with his family, by hijacking his ship. Smalls not only shared prize money for the captured vessel, but was later enrolled as a master in the U.S. Navy.

2. William Tillman: In June of 1861, Tillman, the young Black cook of the schooner *S.J. Waring,* single-handedly recaptured the ship from a prize crew off the Confederate privateer *Jeff Davis,* killing three and capturing three, for which feat, which he is said to have accomplished in little more than seven minutes, Congress awarded him $6,000.00 in prize.

Six Black Men Known to Have Enlisted in the Confederate Army

1. Old Dick, a drummer—and sometime infantryman—in the 18th Virginia.

2. Jacques Esclavon, trooper in Ragsdale's Texas Cavalry Battalion.

3. Gabriel Grappe, trooper in the 6th Louisiana Cavalry.

4. Charles Lutz, private in the 8th Louisiana

5. Jean Baptiste Pierre-August, private in the 29th Louisiana

6. Lufray Pierre-August, private in the 16th Lousiana.

There were undoubtedly other Black men in Confederate service, particularly those who were "passing" before the war, but their names remain unknown.

169

Four Black Camp Servants Who Fought for the South

1. Levin Graham, took up a musket and allegedly "killed four of the Yankees" in an action in late 1861.
2-3. Tom and Overton, joined in several charges at Brandy Station.
4. Peter Vertrees, several times engaged in combat at the side of his Half-Uncle, John Luther Vertrees, an officer in the 6th Kentucky Infantry.

American Indian Soldiers

The Two Seniormost Native American Officers in the War

1. Confederate Brig. Gen. Degataga, a Cherokee chief, more commonly known as Stand Watie, who commanded a brigade of his brethren in the Trans-Mississippi Theater and was the last Confederate general to lay down his arms.
2. Union Col. and Brevet Brig. Gen. Donehogawa, a Seneca sachem generally known as Ely S. Parker, who served as Grant's military secretary, recording the terms of Lee's surrender at Appomattox.

Foreign Soldiers

Seven Noble Foreign Junior Officers Who Served in the Civil War and Then Returned Home

1. Heros von Borck, a Prussian staff officer, obtained leave to go to America in 1861, joined the Confederate Army, rising to become J.E.B. Stuart's chief-of-staff and one of the more unusual characters in the war—he was a huge man who wielded a gigantic sword—before returning home in late 1864. A wholly "unreconstructed" Confederate, von Borck wrote the most comprehensive treatment of the Battle of Brandy Station.

2. Friedrick Wilhelm von Egloffstein, a German baron, came to the U.S. in February of 1862, joined the Union Army, rising to colonel and brevet brigadier before returning home at the end of the war.

3. Felix von Salm-Salm, a Prussian prince and decorated veteran of the First Schleswig-Holstein War, volunteered for the Union in 1861. He served variously as a staff officer and regimental commander (*8th* and later *68th New York*), he mustered out in 1865 as colonel and brevet brigadier general. After the war he served in the *soi disant* Imperial Mexican Army. Eventually returning to Prussia, he fought in the Franco-Prussian War, being killed as a Major of Grenadiers at Gravelotte in 1870.

5. Friedrich Karl von Schirach, a Prussian baron, was visiting his brother, who had migrated to America, when the war broke out. He volunteered for the Union Army, lost a leg in combat, and rose to captain and brevet major. After the he war returned to Germany, where he died within a week of the American entry into World War I in April of 1917, not, unfortunately, too soon to have missed siring the father of Baldur von Schirach, who became the head of the Hitler Youth.

6. Achille de Vecchi, a captain in the Italian Army, secured a year's leave in the Spring of 1862, came to the U.S. and organized the *9th Massachusetts Battery*, which he commanded for sometime, before returning to Italy.

7. Ernst Mattais Peter von Vegesack, a baron, secured leave from the Swedish Army to fight for the Union, serving for a time as aide-de-camp to Maj. Gen. John E. Wool and earning a Medal of Honor in 1863. After the war he returned to Sweden, where he eventually rose to major general.

Foreign Knights-Errant with the Confederate Army

Col. Heros von Borcke (Prussia)

General Prince de Polignac (France)

Col. George Gordon (England)

Col. Bela Estran (Hungary)

Col. Adolphus H. Adler (Hungary)

Maj. Justus Scheibert (Germany)

Col. Karl Friedrich Henningson (Germany)

Augustus Buchel (Germany)

Lord Charles Cavenish (England)

Henry Morton Stanley (England)

Col. Arthur Fremantle (England)

Col. George St. Leger (England)

Foreign Born Confederate Colonels

Belgian

Lt. Col. Henri Honori St. Paul

Lt. Col. Georges Auguste Gaston de Coppens (1st Louisiana Zouaves)

Canadian

Col. William G. Robinson (2nd North Carolina Cavalry)

Cuban

Col. A. J. Gonzalez (Artillery)

English

Col. George Campbell
Col. George Jackson
Lt. Col. George St. Leger Grenfel
Lt. Col. John W. Mallet

French

Lt. Col. Louis Lay (6th Louisiana)
Lt. Col. P.F. de Gournay (12th Battalion Louisiana Artillery)
Col. Aristide Gerard (13th Louisiana)

German

Col. Augustus Reichard (12th Louisiana)
Col. Leon T. von Zincken (20th Louisiana)
Col. Gustav Hoffman (7th Texas Cavalry)
Lt. Col. Victor von Scheliha (Engineers)
Lt. Col. B. F. Eshleman (Louisiana Artillery)
Lt. Col. John P. Emrich (8th Alabama)
Lt. Col. B. W. Frobel (Artillery)
Col. Augustus Buchel (1st Texas Cavalry)

Hungarian

Col. Bela Estvan
Col. Adolphus Adler (Engineers)

Irish

Col. Henry Strong (6th Louisiana)
Col. William Monaghan (6th Louisiana)
Lt. Col. Joseph Hanlon (Louisiana)
Col. A. R. Blakely (Louisiana Artillery)
Col. Jack Thorington (Hilliard's Alabama Legion)
Col. James S. Reily (4th Texas Mounted Rangers)

Lt. Col. Andrew D. Gwynne (38th Tennessee)
Lt. Col. Michael Nolan (1st Louisiana)
Lt. Col. Michael A. Grogan (2nd Louisiana)
Lt. Col. Joseph McGraw (Artillery)
Lt. Col. James A. Nelligan (1st Louisiana)

Polish

Col. Valery Sulakowski (14th Louisiana)
Col. Arthur Grabowski
Col Hypoite Oladowski
Col. Frank Schaller (22nd Mississippi)
Col. Ignatius Szymanski (Louisiana Militia)
Col. Zebulon York (14th Louisiana)

Scottish

Lt. Col. J. G. Campbell (6th Louisiana)
Lt. Col. George H. Morton (2nd Tennessee Cavalry)
Col. James Duff (33rd Texas Cavalry)

Spanish

Col. Santos Benavides (Texas Cavalry)

Swedish

Lt. Col Eric Erson
Col. August Forsberg (51st Virginia)

Foreign Knights Errant With the Union Army

Comte De Paris (France)
Duc de Chartres (France)
Prince de Joinville (France)
Col. Luigi Navone (Italy)
Col. Achille de Vecchi (Italy)
Count Hermann von Haake (Germany)
Col. George W. von Schack (Germany)

Capt. Hubert Dilger (Germany)
Otto von Fritsch (Germany)
Maj. John Fitzroy de Courcy (England)
Baron Ernst von Vegesack (Sweden)
Maj. Adolph Carlsson Warberg (Sweden)
Corfitz Ludwig Joakim Stael, Baron von Holstein (Germany)
Prince Felix Salm Salm (Germany)
Col. Sir Percy Wyndham (England)
Col. Gustave Cluseret (France)
Konstantine Blandowsky (Poland)
Maj. Valentine Bausenwein (Germany)
Henry Bohlen (Germany)
Col. Palle Rosencrantz (Sweden)
Maj. Philip Figyelmassy (Hungary)
Col. Leopold Kazinski (Germany)

Foreign Born Colonels in the Union Army

Austrian

Henry Bornstein (*2nd Missouri*)

Canadian

Joseph R. Scott (*19th Illinois*)

English

Edward D. Baker (*1st California*)
Edward Molineaux (*159th New York*)
James Ashworth (*121st Pennsylvania*)

French

Charles W. Le Gendre (*51st New York*)
Charles A. de Villiers (*11th Ohio*)
Nikolas Greusel (*36th New York*)

German

Adolph E. Buschbeck (*27th Pennsylvania*)
Friederich Hocker (*24th Illinois*)
Leopold von Gilsa (*41st New York*)
Hugo von Wangelin (*12th Missouri*)
August Moor (*28th Ohio*)
Joseph Conrad (*15th Missouri*)
Frederich von Egloffstein (*103rd New York*)
Joseph Gerhardt (*46th New York*)
Fritz Anneke (*34th Wisconsin*)
Ludwig von Blessing (*37th Ohio*)
Carl E. Salomon (*5th Missouri*)
Edward S. Saloman (*82nd Illinois*)
Louis Wagner (*88th Pennsylvania*)
William C. Kuffner (*149th Illinois*)
Albert Sigel (*5th Missouri Militia*)
William Heine (*103rd New York*)
Konrad Krez (*27th Wisconsin*)
George W. Mindel (*27th New York*)

Irish

Patrick Kelly (*88th New York*)
Robert Nugent (*69th New York*)
Richard Byrnes (*28th Massachusetts*)
Thomas Cass (*9th Massachusetts*)
Thomas W. Cahill (*9th Connecticut*)
W. H. Lytle (*10th Ohio*)
James Gwyn (*118th Pennsylvania*)
Patrick H. O'Rorke (*140th Pennsylvania*)
Howard Carroll (*105th New York*)
Michael K. Bryan (*175th New York*)
William J. Sewell (*5th New Jersey*)
Andrew P. Caraher (*28th Massachusetts*)
St. Clair A. Mulholland (*116th Pennsylvania*)
James A. Mulligan (*23rd Illinois*)
Robert H. Minty (*4th Michigan Cavalry*)

George Gray (*6th Michigan Cavalry*)

Italian

Luigi Palma de Cesnola (*4th New York Cavalry*)
Albert C. Maggi (*33rd Massachusetts*)

Norwegian

Hans Christian Heg (*15th Wisconsin*)

Scottish

David Ireland (*137th New York*)

Swedish

Hans Mattson (*3rd Minnesota*)
Oscar Malmborg (*55th Illinois*)
Ernst Holmstedt (*74th United States Colored Troops*)

Swiss

Hermann Lieb (*5th United States Colored Heavy Artillery*)
Samuel Brodbeck (*12th Iowa*)
Arnold Suttermeister (*Artillery*)
Joseph A. Mosch (*83rd New York*)
John H. Kuhn (*145th Illinois*)

Hungarian Officers of High Rank in the Union Army

Maj. General Julius H. Stahel-Szamwald
Brigadier General Alexander Asboth
Col. Anzelm Albert
Col. George Amsberg (*55th New York*)
Lt. Col. Peter Paul Dobozy (*4th U.S. Colored Heavy Artillery*)
Col. John Fiala
Col. Philip Figyelmessy
Col. Cornelius Fornet (*22nd New Jersey*)

Col. Frederick Knefler (*79th Indiana*)
Lt. Col. Gabriel Korpanay (*7th New York*)
Col. Eugene A. Kozlay (*54th New York*)
Col. Geza Mihalotzy (*24th Illinois*)
Col. Joseph Nemeth (*5th Missouri Cavalry*)
Col. Nicholas Perczel (*10th Iowa*)
Lt. Col. Anthony Pokorny (*7th New York*)
Lt. Col. George Pomutz (*15th Iowa*)
Col. Robert J Rombauer (*Missouri Reserve Corps*)
Col. Emery Szabad
Col. George F. Utassy (*39th New York*)
Col. Joseph Vandor (*7th Wisconsin*)
Col. Gustav Waagner (*2nd New York Heavy Artillery*)
Col. Charles Zagonyi
Col. Ladislaus Zsulavsky (*82nd United States Colored Troops*)

Polish Officers of High Rank in the Union Army

Brigadier General Albin Scheopf
Col. Joseph Karge (*1st New Jersey Cavalry*)
Col. Wladimir Krzyzanowski (*58th New York*)
Lt. Col. George O. Sokalski (*26th Missouri*)
Maj. Alexander Raszewski (*31st New York*)
Maj. Ladislaus Koniusjewski (*26th Missouri*)

Jewish Soldiers

Jewish Medal of Honor Winners

Soldier Action	Regiment
Benjamin Levy Glendale	*40th New York Infantry*

Henry Heller Chancellorsville	*66th Ohio Infantry*
David Orbansky Wilderness	*7th Indiana Infantry*
Leopold Karpeles Wilderness	*57th Massachusetts Infantry*
Isaac Gause Berryville, LA	*2nd Ohio Cavalry*
Abraham Greenwalt Franklin	*104th Ohio Infantry*

Highest Ranking Jewish Officers, Union Army

Col. Max Einstein, *27th New York*
Col. Marcus Spiegel, *120th New York*

Female Soldiers

Eight Women Known to Have Enlisted in the Confederate Army

1-2. Mary and Molly Bell, discovered in October of 1864 in Jubal Early's command, having by then served for two years as "Tom Parker" and "Bob Martin."

3. Malinda Blalock, enlisted with her husband in the 26th North Carolina, under the name "Sam Blalock" and served for two months.

4. Amy Clarke, enlisted with her husband, and continued in the ranks after he fell at Shiloh, her sex only being revealed when, on the occasion of a serious wound, she was captured by Union troops, who gave her a dress and sent her South.

5-6. Margaret Henry and Mary Wright, captured in uniform by Union troops in Tennessee in March of 1865.

7. Laura J. Williams, reputedly raised a company of Texans

early in the war in the guise of "Lt. Henry Benford," leading it at Shiloh and in several other actions.

8. Loreta Janeta Velasquez, who may have served, but whose account, *The Woman in Battle*, was based heavily on the adventures of Laura J. Williams.

Note: There were other women detected in the ranks, but none are known by even the fragment of a name.

Sixteen Women Known to Have Enlisted in the Union Army

1. Mary Burns, enlisted in a Michigan regiment, but detected before her company departed for the front.
2. Frances Clalin served in a Missouri militia cavalry regiment.
3. Sara Collins of Wisconsin, but was discovered before her regiment left for the front.
4. Lizzie Compton, enlisted at 14 and served in seven different regiments until seriously wounded.
5. Catherine E. Davidson served in the *28th Ohio*, until wounded at Antietam.
6. Sarah Emma Edmonds, in 1861 as "Franklin Thompson," a male nurse in *Company F, 2nd Michigan*.
7. "Emily," a Brooklynite, mortally wounded whilst serving as a drummer in the *Army of the Cumberland*, at Lookout Mountain.
8. Ellen Goodridge of Wisconsin, she accompanied her fiance into the army, fought by his side for three years, and nursed him through a mortal illness, for which she was disowned by her family.
9-10. Nelly Graves and Fanny Wilson served in the *24th New Jersey* until detected and discharged, after which Ms. Wilson enlisted in the *3rd Illinois Cavalry*.
11. Jennie Hodgers enlisted at the age of 18 in the *95th Illinois*, serving for three years as "Albert Cashier." Never detected, she continued to pass for a man until 1911, when an auto accident led to a hospital stay.
12. Nellie A. K., enlisted with her brother and served with *The Army of the Cumberland* until, her sex being revealed, she was discharged.

13. "The Canadian Low, enlisted in a Missouri regiment in 1862, until arrested for drunkenness.
14. Mary Owens, enlisted with her fiance and served 18 months, until he was killed and she was seriously wounded.
15. Ida Remington, served as an officer's orderly at South Mountain and Antietam, and later with the *11th New York Militia* in the Gettysburg campaign.
16. Mary Wise, served at least two years in an Indiana regiment, for which service she received mustering out pay upon being discovered.

Note: As with the Confederate "soldier girls," there were other women detected in the ranks, but none are known by even the fragment of a name.

Two Women Who Commanded Troops in Action

1. Harriet Tubman, the famed abolitionist and Underground Railroad Conductor, was directly involved in planning a raid along the Combahee River in South Carolina in early June of 1863, and accompanied the expedition, during which she several times suggested to its commander various measures which he thought appropriate for the conduct of the operation.
2. Madam Turchin, wife of Col. Ivan Turchin, "The Mad Russian," led his *19th Illinois* in Tennessee one day in 1862 after he was wounded.

One Woman Regularly Commissioned as an Army Officer

1. Ms. Sally L. Tompkins of Richmond, as a captain of cavalry in the Confederate Army by Jefferson Davis on 9 September 1861, because a hospital which she had established after First Bull Run proved to have a remarkable recovery rate, becoming thereby the only women to hold a regular commission as an officer on either side during the war.

Two Women Commissioned as Contract Surgeons in the U.S. Army

1. Dr. Sarah E. Clapp
2. Dr. Mary E. Walker

One Woman Who Was Awarded the Medal of Honor

1. Dr. Mary E. Walker. A contract surgeon with the Union Army, Dr. Walker's award was revoked in 1916, only to be restored more than 60 years later.

One Woman Chaplain

1. Ella H. Gibson of the Union *1st Wisconsin Heavy Artillery*

Drummer Boys

Six Notable Drummer Boys

1. John Clem, of Newark, Ohio, better known as "Johnny Shiloh" or "The Drummer Boy of Chickamauga, who enlisted at 10 and retired from the Army as a major general in 1916.
2. Jackson, a Confederate camp servant of about 12 or 13, Jackson escaped from slavery and subsequently became a drummer in the U.S. Colored troops.
3. Willie Johnson, from St. Johnsbury, Vermont, was a drummer boy in *Company D* of the *3rd Vermont*, winning the Medal of Honor during the Seven Days, becoming the youngest person to be so honored, being then just about 13.
4. John McClaughlin, a native of Lafayette, Indiana, enlisted as

a drummer in the *10th Indiana* in 1861, being then "a little over ten years of age," and subsequently serving at Forts Henry and Donelson, at Perryville, and other fields, taking a hand with the fighting from time to time.

5. "Little Oirish" was about 11 when he enlisted in the Confederacy's famed "Orphan Brigade" in 1861, serving thereafter at Shiloh, where he helped stem a rout, and on many other fields.

6. Clarence Mackenzie of the *13th New York* was the first member of his regiment to be killed, dying in an accident in the summer of 1861. He was only 10 years old. MacKenzie is a tragic reminder of the multitudes of boys unknown to history who faced death at such an early age.

One Notable Drummer Girl

1. Emily, a young girl from Brooklyn, who was residing in Michigan, at the start of the war she disguised herself as a boy and enlisted in the *Army of the Cumberland*, serving until mortally wounded at Lookout Mountain.

Miscellaneous

Five Men Who Served *Both* Sides

1. Frank C. Armstrong began his Civil War service as a lieutenant in the Union *2nd Cavalry*, fighting at First Bull Run, and not resigning to "go South" until 13 August 1861, thereafter rising to Confederate brigadier general.

2. Manning M. Kimmel, a lieutenant in the U.S. *2nd Cavalry* did not "go south" until shortly after serving at the First Battle of Bull Run.

3. Frank A. Reynolds graduated West Point in June of '61, after the war was well begun, spent several weeks drilling volunteers before being dismissed from the service on 16 July, having been found to have solicited a commission in

the Confederate Army. He later became lieutenant colonel of the 39th North Carolina.

4. Henry M. Stanley joined the Confederate 6th Arkansas in 1861, fighting at Shiloh and, being captured, immediately volunteered for duty with the Union, serving for a while with the army and later joining the navy, before going on to explore Africa.

5. R.K. Meade, Jr., a 2nd lieutenant of engineers and one of the defenders of Ft. Sumter, resigned from the service shortly after the surrender of the fort and accepted a commission in the Confederate Army, but died of natural causes soon afterwards.

The Many Outfits of Edward C. Stockton

A former U.S. Navy officer, Stockton had been expelled from the service for peculation in 1852. When the Civil War broke out he volunteered for Confederate service, again, and again, and again.

1. Lieutenant, South Carolina State Navy, January-May 1861

2. 2nd Lieutenant, Confederate States Marine Corps, May-September, 1861, when he resigned.

3. Civilian, September 1861-January 1862.

4. Captain, 21st South Carolina, January-April 1862

5. Lieutenant, Confederate States Navy, April 1862 to April 1865.

Union Chaplains Killed in Action

Chaplain Action	Regiment
Rev. Arthur B. Fuller Fredericksburg	*16th Massachusetts*
Rev. Orlando N. Benton New Berne	*51st New York*
Rev. John M. Springer Resaca	*3rd Wisconsin*

Rev. Francis E. Butler	25th New Jersey
Suffolk	
Rev. John L. Walther	43rd Illinois
Shiloh	
Rev. Levi W. Sanders	125th Illinois
Caldwell's Ferry	
Rev. John W. Eddy	72nd Indiana
Hoover's Gap	
Rev. Horatio S. Howell	90th Pennsylvania
Gettysburg	
Rev. Thomas L. Ambrose	12th New Hampshire
Petersburg	
Rev. George W. Bartlett	1st Maine Cavalry
Cold Harbor	
Rev. George W. Desnmore	1st Wisconsin Cavalry
L'Angville Ferry	

Six Notable Aeronauts Who Served in the War

1. John Wise
2. John LaMountain
3. Thaddeus Lowe
4. James Allen
5. Ezra Allen
6. Charles Crevor, the only Rebel in the lot.

Five Civil War Mascots

1. "Jeff Davis," a mongrel, was the mascot of the *6th Iowa.*
2. General Lee's Hen, who laid an egg under his camp bed each morning, which provided his breakfast, and whose absence on 4 July 1863, the fourth day of Gettysburg, caused the general considerable grief, until she was located.
3. "Old Abe" was an eagle, the mascot of the *8th Wisconsin,* who served four years in the field, participating in 42 battles, during which he was once wounded. Tethered to a special standard which was borne by the regimental

"Eagle Bearer," "Old Abe" was wont to fly over the heads of the troops, screaming defiance at the enemy.

4. "Old Harvey," a white bulldog, was the mascot of the *104th Ohio*, serving with some distinction at Franklin.

5. "York," a setter, was the pet of Union Brig. Gen. Alexander S. Asboth, and often accompanied his master into action.

6. "Sallie," was the mascot of the *11th Pennsylvania* and is depicted in the unit's monument at Gettysburg.

Four Delicacies Made with Hardtack

1. Hardtack Pudding: Mash hardtack into a fine meal, mix with water and knead into a dough. Fill this with apples or anything else handy, folding it over to cover. Tie the whole thing in a piece of cloth and boil for an hour.

2. Hell-Fire Stew: Boil the biscuits in water and bacon grease until soft enough to eat.

3. Lobscouse: Stew the hardtack with salt meat and vegetables.

4. Skillygalee: Soften the biscuits in water and then fry them in bacon fat until brown.

CHAPTER 7

SOCIETY

Population of the United States in 1860

The States and Territories
Ranked by Population

State	Population	% of U.S. Population
1. New York	3,880,595	12.6%
2. Pennsylvania	2,359,757	7.6%
3. Ohio	2,339,481	7.6%
4. Illinois	1,711,919	5.5%
5. Virginia	1,596,206	5.2%
6. Indiana	1,350,138	4.4%
7. Massachusetts	1,231,034	4.0%
8. Missouri	1,181,992	3.8%
9. Kentucky	1,155,651	3.7%
10. Tennessee	1,109,741	3.6%
11. Georgia	1,057,248	3.4%
12. North Carolina	991,464	3.2%
13. Alabama	964,041	3.1%

14. Mississippi	791,303	2.6%
15. Wisconsin	774,864	2.5%
16. Michigan	742,941	2.4%
17. Louisiana	707,829	2.3%
18. South Carolina	703,620	2.3%
19. Maryland	687,049	2.2%
20. Iowa	674,848	2.2%
21. New Jersey	672,035	2.2%
22. Maine	628,274	2.0%
23. Texas	603,812	2.0%
24. Connecticut	460,131	1.5%
25. Arkansas	434,402	1.4%
26. California	327,263	1.1%
27. New Hampshire	326,073	1.1%
28. Vermont	315,078	1.0%
29. Rhode Island	174,601	0.6%
30. Minnesota	169,654	0.5%
31. Florida	140,423	0.5%
32. Delaware	112,216	0.4%
33. Kansas	107,017	0.3%
34. New Mexico Territory	83,009	0.3%
35. District of Columbia	75,079	0.2%
36. Indian Territory	75,000	0.2%
37. Oregon	52,288	0.2%
38. Utah Territory	40,184	0.1%
39. Colorado Territory	34,277	0.1%
40. Nebraska	28,778	0.1%
41. Washington Territory	11,168	0.0%
42. Nevada Territory	6,857	0.0%
43. Dakota Territory	2,576	0.0%
Total	**30,891,916**	

The States and Territories
Ranked by Black Population

State	Black Population
1. Virginia (C)	548,907
2. Georgia (C)	465,698
3. Alabama (C)	437,770
4. Mississippi (C)	437,404
5. South Carolina (C)	412,320
6. North Carolina (C)	361,522
7. Louisiana (C)	350,337
8. Tennessee (C)	283,019
9. Kentucky (B)	236,167
10. Texas (C)	182,921
11. Maryland (B)	171,131
12. Missouri (B)	118,503
13. Arkansas (C)	111,259
14. Florida (C)	62,677
15. Pennsylvania	56,949
16. New York	49,005
17. Ohio	36,673
18. New Jersey	25,336
19. Delaware	21,627
20. District of Columbia	14,316
21. Indiana	11,428
22. Massachusetts	9,602
23. Connecticut	8,627
24. Illinois	7,628
25. Michigan	6,799
26. California	4,086
27. Rhode Island	3,952
28. Maine	1,327
29. Wisconsin	1,171
30. Iowa	1,069
31. Vermont	708
32. Kansas	627

33. New Hampshire	494
34. Minnesota	259
35. Oregon	128
36. Indian Territory	100
37. New Mexico Territory	85
38. Nebraska	82
39. Utah Territory	59
40. Colorado Territory	46
41. Nevada Territory	45
42. Washington Territory	30
43. Dakota Territory	0
Total	**4,441,893**

A "C" indicates a future Confederate State, a "B" stands for a Border State.

The States and Territories
Ranked by Percentage of Black Population

State	% of Population
1. South Carolina (C)	58.6%
2. Mississippi (C)	55.3%
3. Louisiana (C)	49.5%
4. Alabama (C)	45.4%
5. Florida (C)	44.6%
6. Georgia (C)	44.0%
7. North Carolina (C)	36.5%
8. Virginia (C)	34.4%
9. Texas (C)	30.3%
10. Arkansas (C)	25.6%
11. Tennessee (C)	25.5%
12. Maryland (B)	24.9%
13. Kentucky (B)	20.4%
14. Delaware	19.3%
15. District of Columbia	19.1%
U.S. Average	**14.4%**

16. Missouri (B)	10.0%
17. New Jersey	3.8%
18. Pennsylvania	2.4%
19. Rhode Island	2.3%
20. Connecticut	1.9%
21. Ohio	1.6%
22. New York	1.3%
23. California	1.2%
24. Michigan	0.9%
25. Indiana	0.8%
26. Massachusetts	0.8%
27. Nevada Territory	0.7%
28. Kansas	0.6%
29. Illinois	0.4%
30. Nebraska	0.3%
31. Washington Territory	0.3%
32. Oregon	0.2%
33. Vermont	0.2%
34. Maine	0.2%
35. Iowa	0.2%
36. Minnesota	0.2%
37. New Hampshire	0.2%
38. Wisconsin	0.2%
39. Utah Territory	0.1%
40. Colorado Territory	0.1%
41. Indian Territory	0.1%
42. New Mexico Territory	0.1%
43. Dakota Territory	0.0%

A "C" indicates a future Confederate State, a "B" stands for a Border State.

The States and Territories
Ranked by Number of Slaves

State	Slave Population	% of Black Population
1. Virginia (C)	490,865	89.4%
2. Georgia (C)	462,198	99.2%
3. Mississippi (C)	436,631	99.8%
4. Alabama (C)	435,080	99.4%
5. South Carolina (C)	402,406	97.6%
6. Louisiana (C)	331,726	94.7%
7. North Carolina (C)	331,059	91.6%
8. Tennessee (C)	275,719	97.4%
9. Kentucky (B)	225,483	95.5%
10. Texas (C)	182,566	99.8%
11. Missouri (B)	114,931	97.0%
12. Arkansas (C)	111,115	99.9%
13. Maryland (B)	87,189	50.9%
14. Florida (C)	61,745	98.5%
15. District of Columbia	3,185	22.2%
16. Delaware	1,798	8.3%
17. Indian Territory	100	100.0%
18. Utah Territory	29	49.2%
19. New Jersey	18	0.1%
20. Nebraska	15	18.3%
21. Kansas	2	0.3%
22. California	0	0.0%
23. Colorado Territory	0	0.0%
24. Connecticut	0	0.0%
25. Dakota Territory	0	0.0%
26. Illinois	0	0.0%
27. Indiana	0	0.0%
28. Iowa	0	0.0%
29. Maine	0	0.0%
30. Massachusetts	0	0.0%
31. Michigan	0	0.0%
32. Minnesota	0	0.0%

33. Nevada Territory	0	0.0%
34. New Hampshire	0	0.0%
35. New Mexico Territory	0	0.0%
36. New York	0	0.0%
37. Ohio	0	0.0%
38. Oregon	0	0.0%
39. Pennsylvania	0	0.0%
40. Rhode Island	0	0.0%
41. Vermont	0	0.0%
42. Washington Territory	0	0.0%
43. Wisconsin	0	0.0%
Total	**3,953,860**	**89.0%**

A "C" indicates a future Confederate State, a "B" stands for a Border State.

The States and Territories Ranked by the Number of Free Black Residents

State	# Free Blacks	% Free Blacks: in U.S.	in State
1. Maryland (B)	83,942	17.2%	49.1%
2. Virginia (C)	58,042	11.9%	10.6%
3. Pennsylvania	56,949	11.7%	100.0%
U.S. Average		**11.0%**	
4. New York	49,005	10.0%	100.0%
5. Ohio	36,673	7.5%	100.0%
6. North Carolina (C)	30,463	6.2%	8.4%
7. New Jersey	25,318	5.2%	99.9%
8. Delaware	19,829	4.1%	91.7%
9. Louisiana (C)	18,611	3.8%	5.3%
10. Indiana	11,428	2.3%	100.0%
11. District of Columbia	11,131	2.3%	77.8%
12. Kentucky (B)	10,684	2.2%	4.5%
13. South Carolina (C)	9,914	2.0%	2.4%
14. Massachusetts	9,602	2.0%	100.0%
15. Connecticut	8,627	1.8%	100.0%

16. Illinois	7,628	1.6%	100.0%
17. Tennessee (C)	7,300	1.5%	2.6%
18. Michigan	6,799	1.4%	100.0%
19. California	4,086	0.8%	100.0%
20. Rhode Island	3,952	0.8%	100.0%
21. Missouri (B)	3,572	0.7%	3.0%
22. Georgia (C)	3,500	0.7%	0.8%
23. Alabama (C)	2,690	0.6%	0.6%
24. Maine	1,327	0.3%	100.0%
25. Wisconsin	1,171	0.2%	100.0%
26. Iowa	1,069	0.2%	100.0%
27. Florida (C)	932	0.2%	1.5%
28. Mississippi (C)	773	0.2%	0.2%
29. Vermont	708	0.1%	100.0%
30. Kansas	625	0.1%	99.7%
31. New Hampshire	494	0.1%	100.0%
32. Texas (C)	355	0.1%	0.2%
33. Minnesota	259	0.1%	100.0%
34. Arkansas (C)	144	0.0%	0.1%
35. Oregon	128	0.0%	100.0%
36. New Mexico Territory	85	0.0%	100.0%
37. Nebraska	67	0.0%	81.7%
38. Colorado Territory	46	0.0%	100.0%
39. Nevada Territory	45	0.0%	100.0%
40. Utah Territory	30	0.0%	50.8%
41. Washington Territory	30	0.0%	100.0%
42. Indian Territory	0	0.0%	0.0%
43. Dakota Territory	0	0.0%	0.0%
Total in 1860	**488,033**		

A "C" indicates a future Confederate State, a "B" stands for a Border State.

The States and Territories Ranked by
Smallness of Free Black Population by Percent

State	% of Blacks in State	Number of Free Blacks
1. Indian Territory	0.0%	0
2. Arkansas (C)	0.1%	144
3. Mississippi (C)	0.2%	773
4. Texas (C)	0.2%	355
5. Alabama (C)	0.6%	2,690
6. Georgia (C)	0.8%	3,500
7. Florida (C)	1.5%	932
8. South Carolina (C)	2.4%	9,914
9. Tennessee (C)	2.6%	7,300
10. Missouri (B)	3.0%	3,572
11. Kentucky (B)	4.5%	10,684
12. Louisiana (C)	5.3%	18,611
13. North Carolina (C)	8.4%	30,463
14. Virginia (C)	10.6%	58,042
U.S Average	**11.0%**	
15. Maryland (B)	49.1%	83,942
16. Utah Territory	50.8%	30
17. District of Columbia	77.8%	11,131
18. Nebraska	81.7%	67
19. Delaware	91.7%	19,829
20. Kansas	99.7%	625
21. New Jersey	99.9%	25,318
22. California	100.0%	4,086
23. Colorado Territory	100.0%	46
24. Connecticut	100.0%	8,627
25. Illinois	100.0%	7,628
26. Indiana	100.0%	11,428
27. Iowa	100.0%	1,069
28. Maine	100.0%	1,327
29. Massachusetts	100.0%	9,602
30. Michigan	100.0%	6,799

31. Minnesota	100.0%	259
32. Nevada Territory	100.0%	45
33. New Hampshire	100.0%	494
34. New Mexico Territory	100.0%	85
35. New York	100.0%	49,005
36. Ohio	100.0%	36,673
37. Oregon	100.0%	128
38. Pennsylvania	100.0%	56,949
39. Rhode Island	100.0%	3,952
40. Vermont	100.0%	708
41. Washington Territory	100.0%	30
42. Wisconsin	100.0%	1,171
43. Dakota Territory	0.0%	0

Note: There were no Black inhabitants in the Dakota Territory.

Population of the Confederate States

The Confederate States in Order of Secession

State	Date of Secession
1. South Carolina	20 Dec. 1860
2. Mississippi	9 Jan. 1861
3. Florida	10 Jan. 1861
4. Alabama	11 Jan. 1861
5. Georgia	19 Jan. 1861
6. Louisiana	26 Jan. 1861
7. Texas	1 Feb. 1861
8. Virginia	17 Apr. 1861
9. Arkansas	6 May 1861
10. North Carolina	20 May 1861
11. Tennessee	8 June 1861

The Confederate States
Ranked by Total Population

State	Population
1. Virginia	1,596,206
2. Tennessee	1,109,741
3. Georgia	1,057,248
4. North Carolina	991,464
5. Alabama	964,041
6. Mississippi	791,303
7. Louisiana	707,829
8. South Carolina	703,620
9. Texas	603,812
10. Arkansas	434,402
11. Florida	140,423

The Confederate States
Ranked by White Population

State	White Population
1. Virginia	1,047,299
2. Tennessee	826,722
3. North Carolina	629,942
4. Georgia	591,550
5. Alabama	526,271
6. Texas	420,891
7. Louisiana	357,492
8. Mississippi	353,899
9. Arkansas	323,143
10. South Carolina	291,300
11. Florida	77,746

The Confederate States Ranked by Black Population

State	Black Population
1. Virginia	548,907
2. Georgia	465,698
3. Alabama	437,770
4. Mississippi	437,404
5. South Carolina	412,320
6. North Carolina	361,522
7. Louisiana	350,337
8. Tennessee	283,019
9. Texas	182,921
10. Arkansas	111,259
11. Florida	62,677

The Confederate States Ranked by Order of Secession and Percentage of Blacks in the Population

State	Date of Secession	% Blacks
1. South Carolina	20 December 1860	58.6%
2. Mississippi	9 January 1861	55.3%
3. Florida	10 January 1861	44.6%
4. Alabama	11 January 1861	45.4%
5. Georgia	19 January 1861	44.0%
6. Louisiana	26 January 1861	49.5%
7. Texas	1 February 1861	30.3%
8. Virginia	17 April 1861	34.4%
9. Arkansas	6 May 1861	25.6%
11. North Carolina	20 May 1861	36.5%
13. Tennessee	8 June 1861	25.5%

Population of the Leading Confederate Cities in 1860 (Not Including Slaves)

City	Population
New Orleans	168,675
Charleston	40,578
Richmond	37,910
Mobile	29,258
Memphis	22,623
Savannah	22,292
Norfolk	12,000
Montgomery	8,843

Election of 1860

Electoral Votes of States in 1860 by Section

State	Electoral Votes
Border States	
Kentucky	12
Maryland	8
Missouri	9
Total	**29**
Northern States	
Connecticut	6
Delaware	3
Illinois	11
Indiana	13
Iowa	4
Maine	8
Massachusetts	13

Michigan	6
Minnesota	4
New Jersey	7
New York	35
New Hampshire	5
Ohio	23
Pennsylvania	27
Rhode Island	4
Vermont	5
Wisconsin	4
Total	**178**

Southern States

Alabama	9
Arkansas	4
Florida	3
Georgia	10
Louisiana	6
Mississippi	7
North Carolina	10
South Carolina	8
Texas	4
Tennessee	12
Virginia	15
Total	**88**

Western States

California	4
Oregon	3
Total	**7**

Candidates Running for Election in 1860

Constitutional Union Party

President: John Bell
Vice President: Edward Everett

Northern Democratic

President: Stephen A. Douglas
Vice President: Herschel V. Johnson

Southern Democratic

President: John C. Breckinridge
Vice President, Joseph Lane

Republican

President: Abraham Lincoln
Vice President: Hannibal Hamlin

Popular and Electoral Vote

Popular Vote

Candidate	Popular Votes	% of Vote
Bell	592,906	13%
Breckinridge	848,356	18%
Douglas	1,382,713	29.5%
Lincoln	1,865,593	39.5%

Electoral Vote

Candidate	Electoral Votes	% of Vote
Bell	39	13%
Breckinridge	72	24%
Douglas	12	4%
Lincoln	180	59%

States Carried by Bell

State	Electoral Votes
Kentucky	12
Tennessee	12
Virginia	15
Total	**39**

States Carried by Breckinridge

State	Electoral Votes
Alabama	9
Arkansas	4
Delaware	3
Florida	3
Georgia	10
Louisiana	6
Maryland	8
Mississippi	7
North Carolina	10
South Carolina	8
Texas	4
Total	**72**

States Carried by Douglas

State	Electoral Votes
Missouri	9
New Jersey	3
Total	**12**

States Carried by Lincoln

State	Electoral Votes
California	4
Connecticut	6

Illinois	11
Indiana	13
Iowa	4
Maine	8
Massachusetts	13
Michigan	6
Minnesota	4
New Hampshire	5
New Jersey	4
New York	35
Ohio	23
Oregon	3
Pennsylvania	27
Rhode Island	4
Vermont	5
Wisconsin	5
Total	**180**

The Confederate Goverment

The Davis Administration

President

Jefferson Davis, 1861-1865

Vice President

Alexander Stevens, 1861-1865

Attorney General

Judah P. Benjamin, 1861
Thomas Bragg, 1861-1862
Thomas H. Watts, 1862-1863
George Davis, 1864-1865

Postmaster General

John H. Henninger, 1861-1865

Secretary of the Navy

Stephen R. Mallory, 1861-1865

Secretary of State

Robert A. Toombs, 1861
Robert M.T. Hunter, 1861-1862
Judah P. Benjamin, 1862-1865

Secretary of the Treasury

Christopher G. Memminger, 1861-1864
George A. Trenholm, 1864-1865

Secretary of War

Leroy P. Walker, 1861
Judah P. Benjamin, 1862
George W. Randolph, 1862
Gustavus W. Smith, 1862
James A. Seddon, 1862-1865
John C. Breckinridge 1865

One Country Which Recognized the Confederacy

1. The Duchy of Saxe-Coburg-Gotha

Foreign Born Confederate Leaders of Note

Judah P. Benjamin, b. Virgin Islands. Attorney general, February 1861-September 1861; secretary of war, September 1861-March 1862; secretary of state, March 1862-May 1865.

Christopher Gustavus Memminger, b. Germany. Secretary of the treasury, February 1861-July 1864.

Stephen Russel Mallory, b. British Trinidad. Secretary of the Navy, February 1861-May 1865, the only cabinet officer to keep his position through the war.

Important Jewish Confederate Leaders

Judah P. Benjamin: secretary of war, state, treasury
Abraham C. Myers: quartermaster general of the Confederate Army

One Confederate Public Figure Killed in a "Personal Encounter"

1. Robert E. Ford, the clerk of the *Journal* of the Confederate House of Representatives, killed Robert S. Dixon, the chief clerk of the House in 1863.

The Union Government

Lincoln Administration

President

Abraham Lincoln, 1861-1865

Vice President

Hannibal Hamlin, 1861-1864
Andrew Johnson, 1864-1865

Attorney General

Edward Bates, 1861-1864

James Speed, 1864-1865

Postmaster General

Horatio King 1861
Montgomery Blair, 1861-1864
William Dennison, 1864-1865

Secretary of the Interior

Caleb B. Smith, 1861-1862
John P. Usher, 1862-1865

Secretary of the Navy

Gideon Welles, 1861-1865

Secretary of State

William H. Seward, 1861-1865

Secretary of Treasury

Salmon P. Chase, 1861-1864
William P. Fessenden, 1864-1865
Hugh McCulloch, 1865

Secretary of War

Simon Cameron, 1861-1862
Edwin M. Stanton, 1862-1865

Election of 1864

Popular and Electoral Vote

Popular Vote

Candidate	Popular Votes	% of Vote
Abraham Lincoln (Republican)	2,206,938	55%
George B. McClellan (Democrat)	1,803,787	45%

Electoral Vote

Candidate	Electoral Votes	% of Vote
Abraham Lincoln (Republican)	212	91%
George B. McClellan (Democrat)	21	9%

States Carried By Lincoln

State	Electoral Votes
California	5
Connecticut	6
Illinois	16
Indiana	13
Iowa	8
Kansas	3
Maine	7
Maryland	7
Massachusetts	12
Michigan	8

Minnesota	4
Missouri	11
Nevada	2
New Hampshire	5
New York	33
Ohio	21
Oregon	3
Pennsylvania	26
Rhode Island	4
Vermont	5
West Virginia	5
Wisconsin	8
Total	**212**

States Carried by McClellan

State	Electoral Votes
Delaware	3
Kentucky	11
New Jersey	7
Total	**21**

Women and the War

Five Women Who Were Spies

1. Belle Boyd: a young flamboyant spy for the Confederacy. She used her feminine wiles to cajole military information from important Union military figures. She was reported, arrested and imprisoned several times and even sent beyond Confederate lines twice.

2. Pauline Cushman: an actress turned spy for the Union. She reported on Confederate activities in Tennessee in 1863

before being discovered, arrested and sentenced to hang. Invading Union troops rescued her before the execution could be carried out.

3. Rose O'Neal Greenhow: active in the pre-war Washington social scene, O'Neal was able to attain sensitive information for the Confederacy early in the war. Greenhow's activities were discovered and after a term of imprisonment she was deported to the South.

4. Elizabeth Van Lew: a daughter of a Northern-born wealthy merchant, Van Lew lived in Richmond when the war began. She used an eccentric manner as cover for her espionage activities which even included assisting Yankee prisoners in escaping from Libby Prison. She continued to supply the Federals with information until Richmond was taken.

5. Mary Bowser: a African American slave of the Van Lew family until she was freed by her owners and sent to Philadelphia for an education. Bowser later to returned to Richmond to assist her friend Elizabeth Van Lew in undercover work. At one point, Bowser served as a maid for President and Mrs. Davis and was able to attain secrets from the Confederate Executive Mansion itself.

Six Northern Women Prominent in War Work

1. Louisa May Alcott, served as a nurse, later a noted author.
2. Susan B. Anthony, women's rights advocate, organized the Women's Loyal League.
3. Mary Ann Ball Bickerdyke, a housewife and mother, "Mother Bickerdyke," became a Sanitary Commission worker, beloved of the troops and terror of insensitive officers.
4. Clara Barton, a Patent Office clerk at the start of the war, she went on to serve as a nurse, organized soldiers' relief, and eventually founded the American Red Cross.
5. Dr. Elizabeth Blackwell, the first woman to graduate from an American medical school, helped organize the U.S. Sanitary Commission.
6. Mary Ashton Rice Livermore, a society woman, helped organize the Sanitary Commission and served as its

national director from December of 1862 to the end of the war, becoming thereby the most important woman executive in U.S. history.

Media and the Arts

Thirteen Notable War Correspondents

1. Henry B. Adams, the son and secretary of Charles Francis Adams, U.S. Minister to Britain, and a grandson and great-grandson of Presidents, was for some time a confidential correspondent for *The New-York Times*.
2. Peter W. Alexander, *The Atlanta Confederacy* and *The Mobile Advertiser and Register*.
3. Eugenie Benson, noted "girl" reporter for *Frank Leslie's Illustrated Newspaper*, who sketched the Confederate bombardment of Ft. Sumter and many other actions.
4. Sylvanus Cadwellader, *The New York Herald*.
5. Thomas M. Chester, *The Philadelphia Enquirer*
6. J.R. Hamilton, *The New-York Times*
7. L.A. Hendricks, *The New York Herald*
8. Joseph Howard, Jr., *The New York Times*, later *The Brooklyn Eagle*, perpetrator of the "Great Gold Hoax" of 1864.
9. Karl Marx, various German newspapers
10. E.T. Peters, *The Philadelphia Enquirer*
11. William Swinton, *The New York Times*
12. Frank Vizetelly, *The Illustrated London News*.
13. William H. Russel, *Times of London*

The Eight Most Popular
Confederate Songs of the Civil War
(In no particular order)

1. "Dixie," Dan Emmet
2. "The Bonnie Blue Flag," Henry Macarthy
3. "Lorena," H.D.L. Webster
4. "Maryland, My Maryland," James Ryder Randall
5. "All Quiet Along the Potomac Tonight," Ethel Lynn Beers
6. "When This Cruel War is Over," Charles C. Sawyer
7. "Tenting On the Old Camp Ground," Walter Kittridge
8. "Just before the Battle, Mother," George F. Root

The Dozen Most Popular
Union Songs of the Civil War
(In no particular order)

1. "All Quiet Along the Potomac Tonight," Ethel Lynn Beers
2. "The Battle Cry of Freedom," George F. Root
3. "The Battle Hymn of the Republic," Julia Ward Howe
4. "Lorena," H.D.L. Webster
5. "Marching Along," William B. Bradbury
6. "Marching Through Georgia," Henry Clay Work
7. "Tenting On the Old Camp Ground," Walter Kittridge
8. "We are Coming Father Abraham," James S. Gibbons
9. "Just before the Battle, Mother," George F. Root
10. "John Brown's Body," unknown
11. "Tramp, Tramp, Tramp," George F. Root
12. "When This Cruel War is Over," Charles C. Sawyer

Ten Notable Contemporary Civil War Poems *Not* by Walt Whitman (In no particular order)

1. "Barbara Fritchie," John Greenleaf Whittier
2. "Brother Johnathan's Lament to Sister Caroline," Oliver Wendell Holmes, Sr.
3. "Only a Soldier's Grave," S.A. Jones
4. "Only One Killed," Julia L. Keyes
5. "Somebody's Darling," Marie Ravenel de la Coste
6. "Stonewall Jackson's Way," John W. Palmer,
7. "The Picket Guard," Ethel Lynn Beers, later set to music as "All Quiet Along the Potomac Tonight"
8. "The Portent," Herman Melville
9. "Running the Batteries," Herman Melville
10. "Shiloh, A Requiem," Herman Melville

Ten Notable Contemporary Civil War Poems by Walt Whitman

1. "An Army Corps on the March"
2. "Bivouac on a Mountainside"
3. "Cavalry Crossing a Ford"
4. "Come Up From the Fields, Father"
5. "Oh Captain, My Captain"
6. "Over the Carnage Rose Prophetic a Voice"
7. "When Lilacs Last in the Dooryard Bloomed"
8. "Eighteen Sixty-One"
9. "I Saw an Old General at Bay."
10. "Hush'd be the Camp Today."

CHAPTER 8

AFTER THE WAR

Veterans and Politics

Seven Civil War Veterans
Who Became President

1. Andrew Johnson (1865-1869): Senator from Tennessee before
   the war, Johnson stuck by the Union. Appointed brigadier
   general of volunteers on 4 March 1862, he served as
   military governor of his home state, resigning on 3 March
   1865 to become vice-president, succeeding Lincoln when
   the latter was assassinated on 15 April 1865.
2. Ulysses S. Grant (1869-1877): Appointed lieutenant colonel of
   volunteers on 17 June 1861, Grant rose thereafter to
   lieutenant general and commanding general on 12 March
   1864, and then to full general on 25 July 1866, before
   resigning on 3 March 1869 to become President.
3. Rutherford B. Hayes (1877-1881): Commissioned a major in
   the *23rd Ohio* on 27 June 1861, he rose to brigadier
   general on 19 October 1864, serving creditably as a
   brigade and division commander, most notably in
   Sheridan's Valley Campaign. Elected to Congress in 1864,
   he did not take his seat. Breveted major general on 13

March 1865, he resigned on 8 June to take his seat in the House. Hayes was wounded four times during the war. In 1876 he was elected President.

4. James A. Garfield (1881): Commissioned lieutenant colonel of the *42nd Ohio* on 21 August 1861, and rose steadily through the ranks by distinguished service at Shiloh, and Corinth, and as chief-of-staff of the *Army of the Cumberland*, until he was made a major general of volunteers on 19 September 1863. He resigned shortly thereafter upon being elected to Congress.

5. Chester A. Arthur (1881-1885): Appointed assistant quartermaster general of the New York State militia in 1861, he was responsible for procuring supplies for regiments being raised for both state and Federal service, rising by the war's end to quartermaster general and inspector general, ranking as a major general.

6. Benjamin Harrison (1889-1893): Great-grandson and namesake of Benjamin Harrison, a signer of the Declaration of Independence, and grandson of Indian fighter and ninth President William Henry Harrison, Benjamin Harrison was commissioned as a second lieutenant in the *70th Indiana* on 14 July 1862, and became colonel 24 days later, on 7 August. Harrison led the regiment in the *Army of the Cumberland* at Resaca, Golgotha, New Hope Church, and Peach Tree Creek, Nashville, and during the Carolina Campaign, rising to brigade commander and brevet brigadier general before mustering out on 8 June 1865, to resume his law practice.

7. William McKinley (1897-1901): On 23 June 1861 19 year-old McKinley enlisted as a private in *Company E, 23rd Ohio* (Rutherford B. Hayes' regiment). He served in West Virginia, at Antietam, and in the Shenandoah, rising to captain on 25 July 1864, and brevet major on 13 March 1865, mustering out shortly thereafter.

One Draft Dodger Who Became President

1. Grover Cleveland (Democrat, 1885-1889 and 1893-1897): A

lawyer and Democratic politician in Buffalo, Cleveland provided a substitute when drafted in 1864.

Eight Civil War Veterans
Who Wanted to Be President

1. Union Maj. Gen. George B. McClellan, the erstwhile General-in-Chief and commander of the *Army of the Potomac*, carried the Democratic banner to crushing defeat at the hands of Lincoln in 1864.
2. Union Maj. Gen. Winfield Scott Hancock, a highly successful corps commander in the *Army of the Potomac*, ran as a Democrat and was narrowly defeated by James A. Garfield in 1880.
3. Union Brig. Gen. John W. Phelps lost to Garfield on the Anti-Masonic line in 1880.
4. Union Brig. Gen. Neal Dow also lost to Garfield on the Prohibition ticket in 1880.
5. Union Maj. Gen. Benjamin Butler, one of the most prominent "political generals" in the war, ran on the Greenback ticket in 1884.
6. Union Brevet Brig. Gen. James B. Weaver ran on the Greenback-Labor ticket in 1880 and won the candidacy for the populist People's Party 12 years later.
7. Union Brig. Gen. Clinton B. Fiske tried his luck on the Prohibition line in 1888.
8. Union Maj. Gen. John McC. Palmer, ran on the so-called "Gold Democrat" ticket (with former Confederate Lt. Gen. Simon Bolivar Buckner as his running mate), thereby helping to defeat Democrat William Jennings Bryan's "Free Silver" campaign and elect brevet Maj. William McKinley in 1896.

One Civil War General
Who Didn't Want to Be President

1. Maj. Gen. William Tecumseh Sherman, who enjoyed being

the only full general in the army, declared "If nominated, I will not run, if elected, I will not serve" in 1884.

Generals in Military Action After the Civil War

Five Former Confederate General Officers Who Fought for Imperial Mexico, 1865-1867.

1. Brig. Gen. Mosby M. Parsons, killed in action against the *juaristas* on 15 August 1865.
2. Maj. Gen. Sterling Price
3. Maj. Gen. John B. Magruder
4. Commodore M.F. Maury served for a time as director of the Imperial Observatory.
5. Brig. Gen. Joseph O. Shelby, after first briefly serving with the *juaristas*.

One Union General Who Fought for Republican Mexico, 1865-1867

1. Maj. Gen. Lew Wallace commanded a brigade of volunteers for a time.

One Confederate General Who Became a Cuban Revolutionary Leader

1. Brig. Gen. Thomas Jordan
    In 1869 Jordan joined the Cuban revolutionaries. For a time chief-of-staff of the revolutionary army, he eventually rose to be commander-in-chief, with a $10,000 price on his head. When the Revolution collapsed in 1878 Jordan returned to the United States.

Civil War Generals Who Earned More Fame Fighting Indians

1. Edward Richard Sprigg Canby (1819-1873): Canby fought Confederate invaders in New Mexico before becoming major general of volunteers commanding the Military Division of West Mississippi. Following the war, Canby was made brigadier general and commanded the Department of the Columbia; a colorless and prudent soldier, he became the only Regular Army general ever to be killed by Indians. Warned that Modoc Indians besieged in northern California's lava beds planned to murder him, Canby nevertheless agreed to attend a peace conference unarmed, arguing that he had "never deceived an Indian." On 11 April, two of the peace commissioners were murdered, Canby being shot twice in the head and stabbed in the back. This Good Friday carnage outraged Army and public alike. Today, Indian partisans imply that Canby's murder was somehow his own fault.

2. George Armstrong Custer (1839-1876): A brigadier general at 23, a major general commanding a cavalry division by age 25, the long haired, controversial "Boy General" became lieutenant colonel and *de facto* commander of the *7th Cavalry*, most notably during Sheridan's 1868-69 winter campaign against the Southern Plains tribes. On 25 June 1876, Custer and five *7th Cavalry* companies were annihilated after attacking a huge Sioux-Cheyenne encampment on Montana's Little Bighorn River; the *7th's* remaining seven companies were besieged through the 26th, with total fatalities numbering 268. While General Arthur St. Clair's 1791 defeat by Little Turtle in Ohio had resulted in over twice as many Army deaths, it was "Custer's Last Stand" which became a legend—and, ironically, led to Custer's current and quite unjustified role as the symbolic Indian-hating villain.

3. George Crook (1828-1890): Crook's Civil War posts included commander of the Department of West Virginia and the Army of Western Virginia. Exchanged after capture by the Rebels, he ended the war as a major general of volunteers leading a cavalry division in the *Army of the Potomac*. A notable advocate of mule trains and enlisting Indian auxiliaries from the very tribes being fought, Crook

proved so successful in subduing Apaches that he received an unusual postwar promotion from lieutenant colonel to regular brigadier general. Crooks's performance during the Sioux War of 1876 was less praiseworthy, particularly his strategic defeat at the Battle of the Rosebud, and his 1886 campaign against Geronimo was cut short when his methods displeased commanding general Sheridan. Serving as major general commanding the vast Division of the Missouri in 1888, Crook was active in the Indian Rights Association. When the aged Oglala Sioux chief Red Cloud was informed of Crook's death, he noted sadly, "He, at least, had never lied to us."

4. Nelson A. Miles (1839-1925): Miles took part in all of the major battles of the *Army of the Potomac* save Gettysburg, suffering four wounds and commanding units ranging from regiment to corps before becoming major general of volunteers at age 26. As colonel of the *5th Infantry*, Miles earned Indian-fighting laurels in the Red River War of 1874-75, commanding both infantry and cavalry against Southern Plains tribesmen. After Custer's defeat, Miles helped defeat his friend's slayers with energetic winter campaigning, later vying with General O.O. Howard over credit for defeating the Nez Perce. The efficient but the exasperatingly ambitious Miles replaced Crook as Department of Arizona commander in 1886. During this command, he treacherously induced Geronimo's surrender by deporting peaceful Apaches to Florida. Retired in 1903 as the U.S. Army's last commanding general, Miles died gloriously—collapsing at a circus while saluting the flag as a band played the National Anthem.

5. Ranald S. Mackenzie (1840-1889): Starting the war as an engineer lieutenant, Mackenzie suffered six combat wounds, including the loss of two fingers, accounting for his later Indian name "Bad Hand." Peace found him a major general of volunteers commanding a cavalry division in the *Army of the James*. After reverting to his regular rank of captain, Mackenzie became a colonel commanding Black infantrymen before achieving his greatest renown at the head of the *4th Cavalry*. Mackenzie's exploits in Texas against Comanches, Kiowas, and others included two secretly authorized strikes into Mexico to destroy raiders' sanctuaries. During the Red

River War, Mackenzie won the campaign's only full-scale battle at Palu Duro Canyon, and in the Sioux War of 1876 destroyed Dull Knife's Cheyenne village. Widely considered to be a superb Indian fighter, Mackenzie was promoted to brigadier in 1882, but was forcibly retired due to mental illness in 1884, dying insane in 1889 at age 48.

Four Confederate Generals
Who Served in the War with Spain

1. Maj. Gen. Matthew C. Butler, held the same rank in 1898, and served as one of the American commissioners overseeing the Spanish evacuation of Cuba.
2. Lt. Gen. Fitzhugh Lee, ranked as a major general in 1898, and was commander of *VII Corps*, which undertook occupation duties after the armistice. Had the war lasted longer, Lee would have commanded in the assault against Havana.
3. Brig. Gen. Thomas L. Rosser, was granted the same rank in 1898, but saw no active service.
4. Maj. Gen. Joseph Wheeler, held the same rank in Cuba in 1898, where he bungled the Battle of Las Guasimas.

Nine Union Generals Retreaded
for the War with Spain

1. Maj. Gen. Nelson A. Miles, the commanding general of the Army, had risen from second lieutenant to major general of volunteers by 1865.
2. Maj. Gen. John R. Brooke, a brigadier in '65, served in Puerto Rico.
3. Maj. Gen. John H. Wilson, "boy wonder" cavalryman who was a major general five years after graduating from West Point in 1860, also served in Puerto Rico.
4. Maj. Gen. William R. Shafter, who commanded *V Corps* in Cuba, had emerged from the Civil War as a brevet brigadier general.

5. Maj. Gen. Wesley Merritt, who commanded *VIII Corps* in the Philippines, was a Civil War brigadier general, and had a led a cavalry brigade at Gettysburg.

6. Maj. Gen. Alexander McDowell McCook of the "Fighting McCooks of Ohio," a brigadier general of volunteers during the Civil War, saw no action in 1898.

7. Maj. Gen. Grenville Dodge, who had held the same rank in the civil war, and is more noted as the chief engineer of the Union Pacific, saw no action in 1898.

8. Brig. Gen. Samuel B. Young, who served in Cuba, had a brevet in the same rank from 1865.

9. Brig. Gen. Edwin Vose Sumner, Jr., who also served in Cuba, was a Civil War brevet brigadier.

Six Prominent Naval Heroes of the War with Spain Who Were Civil War Veterans

1. Rear Adm. William T. Sampson, who commanded at Santiago, had done blockade duty during the Civil War, and was aboard the monitor *Patapsco* when she as mined in Charleston harbor in early 1865.

2. Commodore Winfield Scott Schley, who also commanded at Santiago, had also done blockade duty during the Civil War.

3. Commodore George Dewey, the hero of Manila Bay, had been a junior officer on the Mississippi and the East Coast during the Civil War, and fought in a naval brigade at the storming of Fort Fisher.

4. Capt. Charles V. Gridley of Dewey's flagship *Olympia*, had been with Farragut at Mobile Bay.

5. Capt. Charles D. Sigsbee of the ill-fated *Maine*, had been with Farragut at Mobile Bay.

6. Capt. Charles C. Clark, who took the battleship *Oregon* on her famed voyage from the West Coast around South America to join the fleet off Cuba, had also been with Farragut at Mobile Bay.

Passing of the Old Warriors

Five Prominent Confederate Generals Who Died in New York City

1. Maj. Gen. William W. Loring
2. Maj. Gen. Mansfield Lovell
3. Maj. Gen. Gustavus W. Smith
4. Lt. Gen. Richard Taylor
5. Maj. Gen. Joseph Wheeler

More Confederate generals died in New York City than in any other place in the country, 16 of the 425 Confederate generals.

Ten Prominent Union Generals Who Died in New York City

1. Brig. Gen. John M. Brannan
2. Brig. Gen. Richard Delafield
3. Brig. Gen. Thomas C. Devin
4. Maj. Gen. John A. Dix
5. Brig. Gen. Alfred Duffie
6. Brig. Gen. Abram Duryea
7. Brig. Gen. Edward Ferrero
8. Maj. Gen. Schuyler Hamilton
9. Maj. Gen. John Newton
10. Maj. Gen. Franz Sigel

Nearly 12% of the 583 Union generals died in what is now New York City. Those listed here are among the 62 who died within what were the city limits until 1898.

Five Union Generals Who Died in Brooklyn

1. Brig. Gen. Stephen G. Burbridge
2. Maj. Gen. Silas Casey
3. Brig. Gen. Quincy Adams Gillmore
4. Maj. Gen. Henry Slocum
5. Brig. Gen. Max Weber

Ten Prominent Union Generals Buried at West Point

1. Maj. Gen. Robert Anderson
2. Brig. Gen. John Buford
3. Maj. Gen. George A. Custer
4. Maj. Gen. Ethan Allen Hitchcock
5. Maj. Gen. Erasmus D. Keyes
6. Maj. Gen. Judson Kilpatrick
7. Brig. Gen. Ranald S. Mackenzie
8. Maj. Gen. John Newton
9. Maj. Gen. and brevet Lt. Gen. Winfield Scott
10. Maj. Gen. George Sykes

Altogether 18 Union generals are buried at West Point.

All Confederate Generals Buried in Arlington National Cemetery

1. Maj. Gen. Joseph Wheeler
2. Brig. Gen. Marcus J. Wright

Ten Prominent Union Generals Buried in Arlington National Cemetery

1. Maj. Gen. George Crook
2. Maj. Gen. Abner Doubleday
3. Maj. Gen. John Gibbon

4. Brig. Gen. Rufus Ingalls
5. Maj. Gen. Philip Kearny
6. Maj. Gen. Nelson A. Miles
7. Maj. Gen. Edward O. C. Ord
8. Maj. Gen. Daniel Sickles
9. Brig. Gen. John A. Rawlings
10. Maj. Gen. William S. Rosecrans

Just about 10% of all Union generals are buried in Arlington, 58 of 583.

Fifteen Generals Buried in Green-Wood Cemetery, Brooklyn

1. U.S. Brig. Gen. George W. Cullum
2. U.S. Brig. Gen. Richard Delafield
3. U.S. Brig. Gen. Abram Duryee
4. U.S. Brig. Gen. Edward Ferrero
5. C.S. Brig. Gen. Robert S. Garnet
6. U.S. Maj. Gen. Henry Halleck
7. U.S. Maj. Gen. Schuyler Hamilton
8. C.S. Brig. Gen. Nathaniel H. Harris
9. U.S. Brig. Gen. James L. Kiernan
10. U.S. Maj. Gen. Ormsby MacKnight Mitchel
11. U.S. Maj. Gen. Fitz John Porter
12. U.S. Maj. Gen. Henry Slocum
13. U.S. Brig. Gen. Francis Barretto Spinola
14. U.S. Brig. Gen. George C. Strong
15. U.S. Brig. Gen. Thomas W. Sweeny

More Civil War generals are buried at Green-Wood than in any other cemetery except Arlington and West Point. Three other Union generals are buried at other cemeteries in Brooklyn.

One Union General Buried at Annapolis

1. U.S. Brig. Gen. Henry H. Lockwood.
   General Lockwood's unusual resting place derives from the fact

that both before and after the Civil War he was an instructor in mathematics at the Naval Academy.

Civil War Descendants

Five Notable World War II Commanders with Interesting Civil War Ancestors

1. Lt. Gen. Simon Bolivar Buckner, Jr., killed in action on Okinawa in 1945, was the son of Confederate Lt. Gen. Simon Bolivar Buckner.

2. Brig. Gen. Nathan Bedford Forrest III, killed in action over Germany in 1943, was the grandson of Confederate Lt. Gen. Nathan Bedford Forrest.

3. Adm. Husband E. Kimmel, who commanded the Pacific Fleet on 7 December 1941, was the son of Confederate Col. Manning M. Kimmel, who did not "Go South" until shortly after fighting for the Union at First Bull Run.

4. General of the Army Douglas MacArthur was the son of Union Col. Arthur MacArthur, the pair also constituting the only father and son to have earned the Medal of Honor.

5. Gen. George S. Patton, Jr. was the grandson of Confederate Col. George S. Patton, of the 22nd Virginia, killed in action at Winchester, 19 September 1864.

CHAPTER 9

THE CIVIL WAR TODAY

Civil War Nostalgia

The Dozen Best Lines from the Civil War (In chronological order)

1. "Government cannot endure permanently half slave, half free." —Abraham Lincoln, during the Lincoln-Douglas Debates, 1856.
2. "The crimes of this guilty land will be judged away but with blood." —John Brown, on the occasion of his sentence to death, 1859.
3. "No terms except unconditional surrender." —U.S. Grant, during the Henry-Donelson Campaign, 1862.
4. "Come on! Come on! Do you want to live forever?" -Unknown Confederate Colonel, leading a charge at Malvern Hill, 1862.
5. "It is well war is so terrible, we should get too fond of it." —Robert E. Lee, as he observed the field in the aftermath of Fredericksburg, 1862.
6. "The Gettysburg Address," all of it —Abraham Lincoln, 1863.
7. "Damn the torpedoes! Full speed ahead!" —David Glasgow

Farragut, as he ordered the fleet into Mobile Bay, despite the loss of the monitor *Tecumseh* to a mine.

8. "I intend to fight it out on this line if it takes all summer." —Ulysses S. Grant, during the Wilderness Campaign, 1864.

9. "They couldn't hit an elephant at this dis...." —John Sedgwick, as he was hit by a Confederate rifle ball at Spotsylvania, in May 1864, whilst positioning his troops.

10. "There is nothing left for me to do but go and see General Grant, and I would rather die a thousand deaths." —Robert E. Lee, upon deciding that he had to surrender his army, 1865.

11. "The nightmare is gone." —Abraham Lincoln, upon learning that Lee had asked for terms, 1865.

12. "Now he belongs to the ages." —Edwin M. Stanton, upon the death of Lincoln, 1865.

Ten Widely Believed "Facts" About the Civil War Which Are *Not True*

1. Union Maj. Gen. Abner Doubleday invented baseball: Not only did an early version of the game exist in the eighteenth century, popular with, among others, George Washington, but the legend linking the game to Doubleday would have him inventing the game whilst a 19-year old cadet at West Point.

2. Prostitutes are nicknamed "Hookers" after Union Maj. Gen. Joseph Hooker: The usage is well attested long before the Civil War broke out.

3. Robert E. Lee opposed slavery: In several of his letters, Lee expressed considerable support for the institution, and, during the Gettysburg Campaign, made no interference when Confederate troops kidnapped Blacks in Pennsylvania and dispatched them southwards to be sold into slavery.

4. John Wilkes Booth escaped the tobacco warehouse in which he was allegedly killed on 26 April 1861: Few people in America had a higher "recognition" value than Booth, one of the most popular actors of the day, and his body was identified by several highly reliable witnesses, including his dentist and a physician who had once performed

some minor surgery on him, leaving a scar which Booth thought "disfiguring."

5. Lincoln's "Gettysburg Address" bombed: In fact, the crowd greeted the speech with tremendous enthusiasm, and Edward Everett, who had spoken before the President, remarked, "There is more in your two minutes than in my two hours."

6. Confederate observation balloons were made from silk dresses donated by patriotic daughters of the South: Actually the few Confederate balloons which did enter service were manufactured from yard goods. Making them from disassembled dresses would have resulted in numerous small panels of irregular shape, which would have been difficult to sew together and seal.

7. Andrew Johnson was taught to read by his wife: Like most country folk at the time, Johnson had learned to read as a child.

8. U.S. Grant was a drunkard: Actually, Grant appears to have been an occasional binge drinker, a condition brought about by loneliness or inactivity. During the war he was never once drunk when his wife was about or when an operation was in train.

9. Stonewall Jackson died of complications resulting from the amputation of his left arm: At the time of his death, Jackson seems to have been suffering from a severe infection of the pleura or the lungs, brought about by a cold which he had acquired from sleeping on the ground without a blanket on the night of 1-2 May. The stump of his arm and his two other wounds were actually healing nicely at the time of his death.

10. The first Confederate battle flags were made from the undergarments of the South's most beautiful women: While it is true that the first three Confederate battle flags were made by the Cary girls, Hetty and Jennie of Baltimore and their cousin Constance, of Alexandria, allegedly the most beautiful women in the Confederacy, alas for romance, as Constance later observed, "we had no apparel in the flamboyant colors of poppy red and vivid dark blue required."

Civil War Reference Works

Nine Invaluable Civil War Documentary Collections

1. *The Bivouac* (Boston, 1883-1885).
2. *Battles and Leaders of the Civil War* edited by Robert V. Johnson and Clarence C. Buell. Four volumes (New York, 1887).
3. *The Century Magazine* (New York, 1870-1930).
4. *The Confederate Veteran* (Nashville, 1893-1932).
5. *Official Records of the Union and Confederate Navies in the War of the Rebellion.* Thirty volumes (Washington, 1894-1927).
6. *The Rebellion Record* edited by Frank Moore. Eleven volumes (New York, 1861-1864).
7. *Southern Bivouac* (Louisville, 1882-1887).
8. *Southern Historical Society Papers* (Richmond, 1876-1952).
9. *War of the Rebellion...Official Records of the Union and Confederate Armies* edited by the War Department. Seventy volumes in 128 parts. Generally known as the *Official Records.* Also note the companion, *Atlas to Accompany the Official Records of the Union and Confederate Armies.* Three volumes (Washington, 1880-1901).

Eleven Indispensable Old Reference Works on the Civil War

1. *Commanders of Army Corps, Divisions, and Brigades, United States Army, During the War of 1861 to 1865* (Philadelphia, 1887).
2. *Confederate Military History,* edited by Clement Anselm Evans. Thirteen volumes (Atlanta, 1899).
3. Dyer, Frederick H., *A Compendium of the War of the Rebellion.* Three volumes (Des Moines, 1908).

4. Fox, William Freeman, *Regimental Losses in the American Civil War, 1861-1865* (Albany, 1889).

5. Heitman, Francis Bernard, *Historical Register of the United States Army from its Organization, September 29, 1789 to September 29 1889* (Washington, 1890). [Second edition *to March 2, 1903.* Two volumes. Washington, 1903.]

6. Livermore, Thomas L., *Numbers and Losses in the Civil War in America, 1861-1865* (Boston, 1900).

7. *Official Army Register of the Volunteer Force of the United States Army, 1861, 1862, 1863, 1864, 1865.* Eight volumes (Washington, 1865).

8. *Personnel of the Civil War* edited by William Freyne Ammen. Two volumes (New York, 1961). Despite it's relatively recent date, this consists of reprints of several uncirculated War Department documents dating from the turn of the century.

9. The Surgeon General of the United States Army, *Medical and Surgical History of the War of the Rebellion.* Six volumes. (Washington, 1870-1888)

10. *The Union Army: A History of Military Affairs in the Loyal States, 1861-1865.* Eight volumes (Madison, Wisconsin, 1908).

11. Wright, Marcus J., *List of Field Officers, Regiments and Battalions in the Confederate States Army, 1861-1865* (Washington, 1891). As this is almost completely unavailable, only 25 copies having been issued, try Claude Estes' *List of Field Officers, Regiments and Battalions in the Confederate States Army, 1861-1865* (Macon, Georgia, 1912), which was an unauthorized reprint.

Twenty Very Useful Modern Civil War Reference Works

1. Bartleson, John D., Jr., *A Field Guide for Civil War Explosive Ordnance* (Indian Head, Maryland, 1972).

2. Boatner, Mark M., *The Civil War Dictionary.* Second edition (New York, 1979).

3. Brown, John C., *The Civil War Almanac* (New York, 1983).

4. Coggins, Jack., *Arms and Equipment of the Civil War* (New York, 1962).

5. Crute, Joseph H., Jr., *Units of the Confederate Army.* (Gaithersburg, Md., 1988).

6. Edwards, William B., *Civil War Guns* (Harrisburg, Pennsylvania, 1962).

7. Hazlett, James C., *et al.*, *Field Artillery Weapons of the Civil War* (Newark, Delaware, 1983).

8. *The Historical Times Illustrated Encyclopedia of the Civil War*, edited by Patricia Paust (New York, 1986).

9. Hogg, Ian V. *Weapons of the Civil War* (New York, 1986).

10. Krick, Robert K., *Lee's Colonels* (Dayton, Ohio, 1979).

11. Lord, Francis A., *They Fought for the Union* (New York, 1960).

12. Long, Everette Beach, with Barbara Long, *The Civil War Day by Day: An Almanac, 1861-1865* (Garden City, New York, 1971).

13. Neely, Mark E., Jr., *The Abraham Lincoln Encyclopedia* (New York, 1982).

14. Ripley, Warren, *Artillery and Ammunition of the Civil War* (New York, 1970).

15. Rogers, H.C.B., *Confederates and Federals at War* (New York, 1983).

16. Wakelyn, Jon L., *Biographical Dictionary of the Confederacy* (Westport, Connecticut, 1977).

17. Warner, Ezra J., *Generals in Blue.* Second edition (Baton Rouge, 1984).

18. Warner, Ezra J., *Generals in Gray.* Second edition (Baton Rouge, 1983).

19. *Who Was Who in the Civil War* edited by Stewart Sifakis (New York, 1987).

20. Zimmermann, Richard J., *Unit Organizations of the American Civil War* (Paris, Ontario, 1982).

Important Works on the Civil War

A Score of Unusual and Important Recent Works on the Civil War

1. Adams, Michael C.C., *Our Masters the Rebels: A Speculation on Union Military Failure in the East, 1861-1865* (Cambridge, Massachusetts, 1978).
2. Beringer, Richard E., Herman Hattaway, Archer Jones, and William N. Still, Jr., *Why the South Lost the Civil War* (Athens, Georgia, 1986).
3. Blight, David W., *Frederick Douglass' Civil War: Keeping Faith in Jubilee.* (Baton Rouge, 1989).
4. Bussy, John W., and David G. Martin, *Regimental Strengths and Losses at Gettysburg* (Highstown, New Jersey, 1986).
5. Connelly, Thomas L., *The Marble Man: Robert E. Lee and His Image in American Society* (New York, 1977).
6. Current, Richard Nelson, *Those Terrible Carpetbaggers: A Reinterpretation* (New York, 1988).
7. Fishel, Edwin C., "Myths That Never Die," *International Journal of Intelligence and Counterintelligence*, Vol. II, No. 1 (Spring, 1988), pp. 27-58.
8. Frassanito, William A., *Gettysburg: A Journey in Time* (New York, 1975).
9. Glatthaar, Joseph T., *Forged in Battle: The Civil War Alliance of Black Soldiers and White Officers* (New York, 1990).
10. Hattaway, Herman, and Archer Jones, *How the North Won: A Military History of the Civil War* (Urbana, 1982)
11. Linderman, Gerald F., *Embattled Courage: The Experience of Combat in the American Civil War* (New York, 1987).
12. McPherson, James C., *Battle Cry of Freedom* (New York, 1988).

13. McWhiney, Grady, and Perry D. Jamieson, *Attack and Die: Civil War Military Tactics and the Southern Heritage.* (1982).
14. Sutherland, Daniel E., *The Confederate Carpetbaggers* (Banton Rouge, 1988).

The Five Best General Histories of the Civil War

1. *Battle Cry of Freedom* by James M. McPherson (New York, 1988)
2. *The Centennial History of the Civil War* by Bruce Catton, 3 vols. (Garden City, 1961-65)
3. *Ordeal For Union*, 4 vols. and *War For Union*, 4 vols. by Allan Nevins (New York, 1947-71)
4. *The Civil War: A Narrative*, 3 vols. by Shelby Foote (New York, 1974)
5. *How the North Won* by Herman Hattaway and Archer Jones (Urbana, IL, 1983)

Five Valuable Civil War Journals

1. *America's Civil War*: Well illustrated bimonthly covering battles, personalities and special topics, 602 King Street, Ste. 300, Leesburg, VA 22075.
2. *Blue & Gray*: a profusely illustrated, serious bimonthly journal devoted of Civil War history and memorabilia, published by Blue & Gray Enterprises, Box 28625, Columbus, Ohio, 43228
3. *Civil War History*: a scholarly quarterly devoted to the "middle period" of American History, published by The Kent State University Press, Kent, Ohio, 44242.
4. *Civil War Times Illustrated*: an extensively illustrated, well written, serious magazine of the Civil War, appearing ten times a year from Historical Times, Inc., 2245 Kohn Rd, Harrisburg, Pa., 17105-8200.
5. *Military Images*: a bimonthly journal devoted particularly to Civil War era military photographs, frequently with excellent articles on a variety of subjects, published by

Military Images, RDD 2, P.O. Box 2542, East Stroudsburg, PA 18301.

6. *Civil War*: a colorful bimonthly magazine of the Civil War Society which covers all aspects of the War Between the States. Published by Cool Spring Associates, Inc., P.O. Box 770, Berryville, VA 22611.

The Two Funniest Works Ever Written About the Civil War

1. Thomas Connelly, "That Was the War that Was," *The Journal of Mississippi History*, 1968.
2. Karl Marx and Frederick Engels, *The Civil War in the United States* (New York, 1937).

Books on Civil War Personalities

Twelve Excellent Books on Lincoln

1. *Lincoln on Democracy* edited by Mario Cuomo and Harold Holzer (New York 1990)
2. *With Malice Towards None: The Life of Abraham Lincoln* by Stephen B. Oates (New York, 1977)
3. *Lincoln the President*, 4 vols. by James G. Randall (New York, 1945-55)
4. *Lincoln and His Generals* by T. Harry Williams (1952)
5. *Abraham Lincoln: A History*, 10 vols. by John G. Nicolay and John Hay (New York, 1890)
6. *Lincoln and the Second American Revolution* by James M. McPherson
7. *The Abraham Lincoln Encyclopedia* by Mark E. Neely (New York, 1982)

8. *Lincoln at Gettysburg: The Words that Remade America* by Gary Wills (New York, 1992)

9. *Abraham Lincoln: The Prairie Years*, 2 vols. (New York, 1926)and *Abraham Lincoln: The War Years*, 4 vols. (New York, 1939) by Carl Sandburg

10. *Lincoln's Quest for Union: Public and Private Meanings* by Charles B. Strozier (New York, 1982)

11. *Abraham Lincoln Laughing: Humorous Anecdotes From Original Sources by and About Abraham Lincoln* (Berkley, CA 1982) by P.M. Zall

12. *The Lincoln Nobody Knows* by Richard N. Current (New York, 1958)

Ten Interesting Autobiographies by Prominent Civil War Figures

1. *Personal Memoirs of U.S. Grant* (New York, 1885)

2. *Memoirs of W.T. Sherman* (New York, 1887)

3. *From Manassas to Appomattox* by James Longstreet (Philadelphia, 1903)

4. *Narrative of Military Operations...during the Late War Between the States* by Joseph E. Johnston (New York, 1874)

5. *Reminiscences of the Civil War* by John B. Gordon

6. *Destruction and Reconstruction* by Richard Taylor (New York, 1879)

7. *Personal Memoirs of P.H. Sheridan* (New York, 1888)

8. *Life and Letters of G. Gordon Meade* (New York, 1913)

9. *McClellan's Own Story* (New York, 1886)

10. *The Rise and Fall of Confederate Government* by Jefferson Davis (New York, 1881)

Books on Campaigns and Battles

The Ten Best Campaign Studies

1. *The Campaign of Chancellorsville*, by John Bigelow, Jr. (1910)
2. *The Gettysburg Campaign*, by Edwin B. Coddington (1968)
3. *Stonewall in the Valley*, by Robert G. Tanner (1976)
4. *Landscape Turned Red*, by Stephen W. Sears (1983)
5. *Chickamauga*, by Glenn Tucker (1961)
6. *Lee's Last Campaign*, by Clifford Dowdey (1960)
7. *The Vicksburg Campaign*, by Edwin C. Bearss (1985-1986)
8. *If It Takes All Summer, The Battle of Spotsylvania*, by William D. Matter. (1988)
9. *To Appomattox*, by Burke Davis (1959)
10. *The Red River Campaign*, Ludwell H. Johnson (1958)

The Ten Best Gettysburg Books

1. *The Gettysburg Campaign: A Study in Command*, by Edwin B. Coddington (1968)
2. *Gettysburg: The Second Day*, by Henry W. Pfanz (1987)
3. *The Cavalry at Gettysburg*, by Edward G. Longacre (1986)
4. *The Attack and Defense of Little Round Top*, by Oliver W. Norton (1913)
5. *Pickett's Charge*, by George R. Stewart (1913)
6. *The Guns at Gettysburg* by Fairfax Downey (1958)
7. *Regimental Strengths and Losses at Gettysburg* by John W. Busey and David G. Martin (1986)
8. *Here Come the Rebels!*, by Wilbur S. Nye
9. *Lee and Longstreet at Gettysburg*, by Glenn Tucker (1968)

10. *Crisis at the Crossroads: The First Day at Gettysburg,* by Warren W. Hassler, Jr. (1970)

Unit Histories

The Ten Best Confederate Unit Histories

1. *A Southern Record: The Story of the 3rd Louisiana Infantry,* by W.H. Tunnard (1866)
2. *"Co. Aytch," A Side Show of a Big Show,* by Sam Watkins (1882)
3. *The Stonewall Brigade,* by James I. Robertson, Jr. (1963)
4. *The Bloody Sixth North Carolina,* by Richard W. Jobst (1965)
5. *The Orphan Brigade,* by William Davis (1980)
6. *Lee's Tigers, The Louisiana Infantry in the Army of Northern Virginia,* by Terry L. Jones (1987)
7. *Hood's Texas Brigade: Lee's Grenadier Guard,* by Harold S. Simpson (1970)
8. *History of Kershaw's Brigade,* by D. Augustus Dickert (1899)
9. *In Camp and Battle with the Washington Artillery,* by William Owen (1885)
10. *A History of the Laurel Brigade,* by William M. McDonald (1907)

The Ten Best Union Unit Histories

1. *The Twentieth Maine* by John J. Pullen (1957)
2. *The Twenty-Fourth Michigan of the Iron Brigade,* by Donal L. Smith (1962)
3. *Service with the Sixth Wisconsin Volunteers,* by Rufus R. Dawes (1890)
4. *To Gettysburg and Beyond: The Twelfth New Jersey Volunteer Infantry,* II Corps, Army of the Potomac, 1862-1865, by Edward Longacre (1988)
5. *The Iron Brigade,* by Alan T. Nolan (1961)

6. *History of the Thirteenth Regiment of Connecticut Volunteers*, by Homer B. Sprague (1867)
7. *The Story of the Sherman Brigade*, by Wilbur F. Hinman
8. *History of the Twelfth Regiment New Hampshire Volunteers*, by Asa W. Bartlett (1897)
9. *History of the First Maine Cavalry*, by Edward B. Tobie (1887)
10. *Berdan's U.S. Sharpshooters in the Army of the Potomac*, by Charles A. Stevens (1892)

Civil War Fiction

The Best Civil War Novels

1. *The Killer Angels*, by Michael Shaara (1974)
2. *The Red Badge of Courage*, by Stephen Crane (1895)
3. *Andersonville*, by MacKinlay Kantor
4. *Traveller*, by Richard Adams
5. *Shiloh*, by Shelby Foote
6. *Gone With the Wind*, by Margaret Mitchell (1936)
7. *The Crater*, by Richard Slotkin (1980)
8. *The History of Rome Hanks and Kindred Matters*, by Joseph S. Pennell (1944)
9. *Bugles Blow No More*, by Clifford Dowdey (1937)
10. *Unto This Hour*, by Tom Wicker

Nine Unusual Recent Works of Civil War Fiction

1. Adams, Richard, *Traveler* (New York, 1988).
2. Auchincloss, Louis, *Watchfires* (Boston, 1982).
3. Brown, Rita Mae, *High Hearts* (Toronto/New York, 1986).
4. Jones, Douglas C., *Elkhorn Tavern* (New York, 1980).
5. Rising, Clara, *In the Season of the Wild Rose* (New York, 1986).
6. Safire, William, *Freedom* (Garden City, New York, 1987).

7. Slotkin, Richard, *The Crater* (New York, 1980).
8. Vidal, Gore, *Lincoln* (New York, 1984).
9. Willis, Connie, *Lincoln's Dreams* (Toronto and New York, 1987).

Civil War Board Games

Richard Berg's Lists of The Best Civil War Board Games

As of the beginning of 1992 there were rather more than 125 titles that could qualify as Civil War board games. However, some were either so old they had passed into legend or so obscure that not even their publisher knows they exist. Some eyebrows may be raised because several of the games on the lists are my own. However, of the more than 125 games published, almost 20% are mine, which makes including some of them somewhat unavoidable. Moreover, while four of the best are my designs [a case of objective subjectivity], two of the worst can also be laid at my doorstep. For those of you new to this sort of thing—and perhaps interested in trying one out—I have rated the complexity of the good games from "1" (very simple) to "10" (denser than the Manhattan Project).

The Ten Best Civil War Board Games

1. *1863*, published by GMT (1991). [4]
2. *A House Divided*, published by GDW (2nd edition, 1989). [3]
3. *Barren Victory*, published by The Gamers (1991). [7]
4. *Chickamauga*, published by SPI/TSR (2nd edition, 1984). [2]
5. *Corinth*, published by SPI, 1981. [7]
6. *First Blood*, published by Simulation Design, Inc., 1990. [8]
7. *Manassas*, published by Iron Crown (3rd edition, 1981). [5]

8. *South Mountain*, published by West End Games, 1984. This was voted Best Game of 1984. [5]
9. *Terrible Swift Sword*, published by SPI/TSR (2nd edition, 1986). [8]
10. *The Civil War*, published by Victory Games (1983). [7]

Contributors

Richard H. Berg has designed over forty historical wargames, of which three were voted "Best Game of the Year." In 1988 he was awarded a special *Charles Roberts Award* for Lifetime Achievement. Mr. Berg also publishes *Berg's Review of Games*.

John Cannan is author of *The Antietam Campaign, The Atlanta Campaign* and *The Wilderness Campaign*. He has also edited two books in the *Eyewitness to the Civil War* series.

Richard L. DiNardo holds a doctorate in military history. He is a Professor of History at St. Peter's College, New Jersey, and is the author of a book and several articles on the Civil War and military history.

David Martin has written numerous books on various aspects of the Civil War, including *The Vicksburg Campaign, Jackson's Valley Campaign, The Shiloh Campaign* and *Confederate Monuments at Gettysburg*. He has also authored many articles on military history and designed eight simulation games. He currently teaches in New Jersey.

Albert A. Nofi, who holds a doctorate in military history, is the author of over a dozen books, including *The Alamo* and *The Gettysburg Campaign*, and numerous articles in military history, the designer of a number of notable military simulation games, and one of the editors of this volume.

Wayne Michael Sarf, a student at the City University of New York Graduate Center is the author of *God Bless You, Buffalo Bill: A Layman's Guide to History and Western Film* (1983) and *The Little Bighorn Campaign*(1992). He has also contributed numerous reviews and articles to magazines ranging from *Film Comment* to *American Spectator*.

Kathleen B. Williams, who has taught at Sophia University in Tokyo and Panama Canal College, is the author of several articles in military history, a field in which she is a doctoral candidate at the Graduate School of the City University of New York.